THE NAKED IRISH:

PORTRAIT OF A NATION BEYOND THE CLICHÉS

CLARE O'DEA

RED STAG

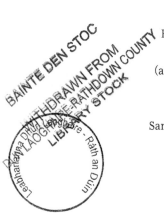

First published in 2019
RED STAG
(a Mentor Books imprint)
Mentor Books Ltd
43 Furze Road
Sandyford Industrial Estate
Dublin 18
Republic of Ireland

Tel: +353 1 295 2112/3
Fax: +353 1 295 2114
email: admin@mentorbooks.ie
website: www.mentorbooks.ie / www.redstag.ie

A CIP catalogue record for this title is available from the British Library.

ISBN 978-1-912514-51-9

Bergli Books grants Mentor Books the right to use cover art and design from Clare O'Dea's *The Naked Swiss* for the cover of *The Naked Irish*, published by Red Stag.

Contents

For my mother, Máire

ACKNOWLEDGEMENTS

It has been a pleasure to encounter so much generosity and kindness while researching and writing this book. I would particularly like to thank John O'Hagan, Ailbhe Smyth, Claire Hamilton, Paul McVeigh, Piotr Mach, Ida Milne, Pat Jourdan, Father Conor McDonogh, David Rice, Conor Kostick, Teresa Donnellan, Sinéad Grace and Peter O'Connell for their time and expertise. Special thanks to Laura and Greig in Belfast and Joy in Dublin for their warmth and openness.

I received invaluable feedback on early drafts from Kim Hays, Una McCaffrey, Jessica Dacey, Marius Schutz, Sarah Moore Fitzgerald and Padraig Rooney. Thank you for your help.

For lighting the way on this writing journey, thanks to Máire O'Dea, Jennifer O'Dea, Ben Moore, Victoria Bruce, Niall McArdle, Tara McLaughlin Giroud, Helen O'Dea, Thomas O'Dea and Ruth O'Dea. I am very grateful to Liz Nugent and John Boyne for their collegial support.

Warm thanks to all the publishing team at Red Stag, in particular my editor Treasa O'Mahony who worked on the book with great skill and good humour. I am very grateful to Daniel McCarthy for believing in this project from the beginning.

I was fortunate to have access to the facilities and books at dlr Lexicon library and the Bibliothèque cantonale et universitaire de Fribourg during my research. As a writer, I could not manage without this important public service.

My daughters, Maeve, Ciara and Ashley, have been brilliant throughout the writing process. I hope this book enriches their understanding of being Irish. Finally, *merci vielmal* to my husband Thomas for always having faith in me.

The publishers wish to thank the following:
PA photos/Niall Carson; Getty Images; Photocall Ireland; RTÉ Archives; Allergan Pharmaceuticals; Tony Hawk; *The Dublin Review*; Martin Malone

FOREWORD

Irish identity was constructed from the outside. When the Irish fully entered the English-speaking world in the mid-19th century, the door closed behind them. From that point on, we would be defined by our position as bit players in that world, dominated by the two cultural giants, the British and the Americans.

So the Irish became the surly servants, the rowdy drunks, the simple peasants, the cute hoors, the religious fanatics, the rebels, the entertainers – essentially the other. These reductive labels applied at home and abroad.

The green-tinged mirror still reflects back many of these old stereotypes, but there is no need for us to keep gazing in that direction. How much more interesting it is to be the protagonist of your own story.

As we approach a century of independence, it is time to consider whether the old clichés and stereotypes are fit for purpose. Is it possible to imagine a truer, fairer and healthier Irish identity? I believe it is, and this book is my contribution to that process, which is already under way.

In school, we learnt one sad story after another, tales of dashed hopes and doomed endeavours, from the Flight of the Earls to 1916. Everything was supposed to change with independence, but it hasn't been a straight trajectory. The fractured North weighs us down. Peace was a long time coming, and prosperity, when it finally came along, hit the country like a roaring flood, leaving us in a sea of mud.

On the positive side, we have much to celebrate. After the setback of the last crash, we have regained our economic power. Beginning in the 1960s, we gifted ourselves free education and we have used it well. We are not fearful of losing our heritage, and we (mostly) understand that sharing it with the new Irish makes it stronger. Piece by piece, we broke the hegemony of the Catholic Church and banished shame. We are in a better place, and, on the whole, we like who we have become.

In the Irish story, we cannot change the beginning, but we can change the ending. Membership of the European Union has been transformative for Ireland. Isolation didn't suit us. A more progressive definition of nationhood has freed us from old prejudices, from narrow definitions of identity, from borders.

Being Irish means negotiating the gap between the romance and the reality of the nation. It means confronting our failings and trying to rectify them. Ireland has always seemed like an unfinished project with a long snag list. Things have got better, a lot better, but the country is still a work in progress.

It is important to question the most common assumptions about the Irish that have endured to the present day. Do these stereotypes stand up to scrutiny? If we strip away the layers of exaggeration, can we find the kernel of truth? And what can we learn from the exercise?

In this book, I will take one stereotype at a time and give it the stress test. Are the Irish a nation of emigrants if we have the second highest foreign-born population in Europe? Are we Catholic if attendance at Mass is as low as two percent in some parishes? Do we really hate the English and want a united Ireland? Is the oppression of women in our DNA? Are the Irish really friendly or just faking it?

In my quest to answer these questions, I have set out to rediscover my fellow countrymen and women and assembled the available evidence. Having lived two thirds of my life in Ireland and one third abroad, I have done this through the lens of someone who exists in an in-between place, part-outsider, part-insider. The result, I hope, is to paint a true picture of modern Ireland.

There is a joy in being Irish. It lies in the affection we feel for the community, and for our flawed nation, the pleasure we take in our identity, our culture and our delightful landscape. Anyone who feels Irish knows this joy. It is the best basis from which to recraft the Irish identity. All we have to do is open the door.

Clare O'Dea

CHAPTER 1

The Irish are a Nation of Emigrants

'Emigration was not unique to Ireland. But the type of emigration, the scale of emigration, and the impact of emigration were. In no other European country was emigration so essential a prerequisite for the preservation of the nature of the society.' [i]   J.J. Lee, historian, 1989.

'In terms of actual citizens abroad, it is estimated that there are approximately 1.47 million citizens resident outside the State.' [ii]

Department of Foreign Affairs Irish Abroad Unit, 2017.

'The alien home may have gems and gold,
Shadows may never have gloomed it;
But the heart will sigh for the absent land
Where the love-light first illumed it.'

John Locke, *Dawn on the Irish Coast*, 1877.

The emigrants' ship is leaving and all the young people on board are trying to keep sight of their heartbroken parents, waving forlornly on the quayside. Our pale and anxious heroine, Eilis, played by Saoirse Ronan, is having a peak pale and anxious moment as she stands on the deck of the ship that will take her away from everything and everyone she knows and loves. Green coat smartly buttoned up, new passport clutched in her hand, she is fleeing the narrow minds and narrow opportunities of 1950s Ireland.

In the film adaptation of Colm Tóibín's novel *Brooklyn*, the image of the lonely emigrant girl blowing a last kiss to her sister is perfectly crafted to tug at the heartstrings of Irish and American audiences alike.

The quayside farewell is not featured in the novel, but in the movie this parting scene is essential. Leaving home is, famously, the speciality of the Irish, the prelude to longing for home, our other speciality. Half of our songs are about the lost homeland.

And there is a good reason for this. Ireland produced more emigrants per capita than any other European country during the 'age of mass migration' to the New World, between the mid-19th century and the beginning of the First World War.

In that phase of emigration, four out of five Irish emigrants went to the United States. Most of the emigration could be categorised as forced to some degree, from victims of eviction and hunger to economic migrants with no prospects at home. Particularly around the time of the Great Famine (1845-1848), emigration for the Irish was a traumatic experience, a mass movement of the dispossessed.

But *Brooklyn* is set in the 1950s, 30 years after independence and a century after the famine. Hunger and persecution were gone but other pressures came into play as the 1950s became the worst decade in the 20th century for Irish emigration. Some 15 per cent of the population took the boat, at that time mostly to Britain. It would not be until 1996 that Ireland made the transition from net emigration to sustained net immigration for the first time.

Top of the tree

Brooklyn is just one example of an entire genre of Hollywood movies romanticising the plucky Irish emigrant, from *Little Annie Rooney* (1925) to *The Sullivans* (1944) to *Far and Away* (1992).

We also do our share of romanticising at home. Who didn't love President Mary Robinson's idea to put a candle in the window for emigrants? Every Christmas the television cameras go to the airports to capture emotional scenes of families being reunited, tapping into the old narrative of grievance at what we poor Irish have to suffer. But the world has changed, as has Ireland's place in it. The job of honestly distinguishing the current Irish experience of emigration from the past exodus has yet to be completed.

Though emigration hasn't gone away, the scale of people leaving Ireland and the personal cost involved has diminished. Irish emigrants now travel by plane, their paperwork is in order, they have good qualifications and job prospects and no-one is campaigning in the destination countries to keep their kind from coming. In the hierarchy of world migration, Irish emigration is a comfortable experience, near the top of the tree.

In 2018, the UN Refugee Agency reported that around the world 44,000 people a day were forced to leave their homes because of conflict and persecution, bringing the total number of forcibly displaced people to more than 70 million, the highest level of displacement in history. In an age when boat people are banished to the island of Nauru off the Australian coast or left to drown in the Mediterranean Sea, when the US army is dispatched to the southern border to demonise poor and persecuted arrivals, and when construction workers suffer human rights abuses building arenas for sports events to which Irish people travel for leisure, no-one can claim the tragic mantle for Ireland anymore.

Irish emigrants have 'influenced and shaped the world', EPIC The Irish Museum of Emigration in Dublin reminds us. Neville Isdell, the museum's founder (and former Chairman and CEO of Coca Cola), is a shining example, having pursued a successful career working in more than half a dozen countries. The interactive museum brings to life the stories of the diaspora: Irish workers, soldiers, doctors, scientists, entertainers and missionaries, the famous few and the forgotten millions, who contributed their life's work to other countries.

How fitting and yet how extraordinary it is that Ireland is now being influenced, shaped and enriched by new people. In the space of one generation, Ireland has also become a nation of immigration. It is a fact of economics that a growing economy attracts new workers who become net contributors. At 17.3 per cent, Ireland has the second highest foreign-born population in Europe, mostly due to recent immigration. Our 'never forget' attitude to our own history of emigration has undoubtedly influenced the reception of immigrants here. It has its uses – empathy is definitely better than self-pity.

In comparison to its European counterparts, Ireland is now a country of large-scale immigration, but without any long-term experience of dealing with integration. In theory that could have been a recipe for disaster but the transition has happened without social unrest. Ireland has begun immigration with a clean slate and no compulsion to make the same mistakes as others. Without a history of stigmatising immigrants or blaming them for all social ills, the Irish and new residents have been able to skip a lot of unnecessary unpleasantness. We had social ills before we had immigrants so we realise the two don't go together. There is no political capital to be gained from bad-mouthing immigrants, as those who have tried to start new parties playing this card have discovered.

However, racism is still a problem in everyday life. Two empty hotels in Donegal and Roscommon, earmarked for accommodation for asylum seekers, were damaged in arson attacks within the space of three months between November 2018 and January 2019. But most racist attacks never make it into the crime statistics. The European Network Against Racism (ENAR) Ireland collects information on racist incidents through its online reporting system, iReport.ie. The most common types of incidents reported were patterns of ongoing harassment, followed by assaults and threats to kill or harm and other forms of threats. In its latest report, ENAR lists one case where a woman pulled a Muslim schoolgirl's veil from her face and slapped her glasses off as she roared abuse at her on a city street. In another incident, an African man was accused of theft (of his own mobile phone) in a post office queue and told by staff – untruthfully – that the Gardaí had been called. These are just two incidents out of 596 reported in 2017. For more on this subject, see **Chapter 10: The Irish are Friendly**.

Slow burner

Emigration has always been a barometer for the Irish economy. Independent Ireland continued to produce economic migrants in significant numbers all the way up to the 1980s. After the large waves of emigration to the US were curtailed by the Great Depression (1929 – 1939), Britain became the prime destination for more than 80 per cent of Irish emigration. Ireland and Britain shared a common travel area which meant no logistical barriers to Irish citizens, mainly unskilled workers, crossing the Irish Sea.

A policy of economic protectionism, initiated by the Irish government in the 1930s and compounded by a trade war with the United Kingdom (1932 to 1938), blocked growth and left Ireland in a weak position by the beginning of the Second World War. Irish workers naturally flocked to the UK to fill the labour gap during the war. A further 70,000 from the Republic enlisted as volunteers in the British Armed Forces.

The post-war recovery that swept through Europe skipped Ireland entirely. By the 1950s, emigration had reached almost 50,000 a year out of a population of 2.9 million. People sincerely feared for the viability of the country. My Galway grandfather ended up emigrating to the north of England to work in the building trade, in the hope of keeping his family in Ireland. It was meant to be a temporary measure, and he did eventually return for good when times got better. But by leaving Ireland for work, he beat a path that his four sons would follow. In many rural areas, emigration was the default at school-leaving age; too many young people, like my uncles, had better links to work opportunities in Britain than in their own country.

Times got better thanks in large part to a five-year economic development plan drawn up by the civil servant Ken (TK) Whittaker and promoted by Seán Lemass, Fianna Fáil Taoiseach from 1959 to 1966. The plan, which did away with protectionist structures and opened up Ireland to foreign investment, was widely accepted by industry, agriculture and unions. Ironically, Lemass was the same man who had first implemented protectionism as minister for industry and commerce in the 1930s. The decision to invest in human capital came later with the 1967 Free Education Act. This transformed prospects for poorer families, opening the door to free secondary schooling for all.

Whittaker's plan stimulated modest growth in the early 1960s which accelerated later in the decade and on into the early 1970s, helped along by the anticipation of EEC membership, which came about in 1973. Emigration was temporarily outstripped by immigration (mostly returned emigrants) during this period, allowing long-awaited population growth. Incomes rose, outpacing growth in Britain and Northern Ireland. By 1974, new industry, attracted by generous tax breaks and subsidies, accounted for over 60 per cent of industrial output.

A combination of bad luck and bad governance interrupted this momentum so that the 1980s were again a struggle, with net emigration of 200,000 over the decade. My best friend emigrated to Canada with her family in 1985, a separation I experienced like a bereavement. And as my older cousins came up to the age of emigration, they made tracks, one by one, to Boston and London. After the more upbeat 1960s and 1970s, we seemed to be doomed to remain the emigrant nursery.

And then, somewhere in the mid-1990s, the economy gobbled a handful of amphetamines, and the habit of many lifetimes was finally broken. The turning point was 1996, the first year of net-immigration that became sustained. Ireland was the last country in the European Union to display this trend. But just when we had almost forgotten the language of leaving, the economic crash of 2008 brought another smaller and shorter wave of Irish emigration. More about that turn of events later in the chapter.

Double standard

In another scene from *Brooklyn*, a few months into her new life in New York, Eilis is helping out at a charity Christmas dinner for Irish men down on their luck. The shabbily-dressed men queuing up for their turkey and ham have a defeated air about them.

The kindly priest who organised Eilis's passage to America from Ireland as well as her accommodation and job (they don't make 'em like they used to) tells her, his voice charged with sadness: 'These are the men who built the tunnels, the bridges, the highways. God alone knows what they live on now'. There is a brief interlude of merriment and bottles of porter being consumed before someone gets up to sing a *sean nós* song. In slow motion, the camera passes from face to craggy face, tears glistening in the eyes of the poor

Engraving of Emigrants leaving Ireland by Henry Doyle (1868).[iii]

Irish labourers and our heroine, the kind helper, as they are overcome by mournful yearning for the old country.

For many second and subsequent generation Americans, some of them comfortably at home with present-day anti-immigrant sentiment, this is the kind of immigration they can get behind. Immigration as it is supposed to be: noble, white and in the past. Most importantly it celebrates their identity and confirms their sense of being special and deserving, a reminder that their ancestors paid their dues in heartache for the good fortune many Irish Americans enjoy today.

Bill O'Reilly, a multi-millionaire media personality who caused his employers (primarily Fox News) to pay out massive settlements in sexual harassment lawsuits against him, came to Ireland on a summer visit in July 2018 and took the time to score some political points with his holiday snaps on Twitter.

'Enjoying my time in Ireland. Visited County Cavan where my ancestors were evicted from their land in 1845. That forced them to come to America legally so they wouldn't starve. Pardon me if I reject the 'white privilege' scenario if applied to my family.'

A powerful, wealthy man – albeit disgraced – using distant ancestry of hardship and 'legal' immigration to dismiss the accrued benefits of generations of white American life. If only his was an isolated case.

There is something to be unpicked about Irishness and whiteness. The Irish overwhelmingly emigrated to white-controlled or white-majority countries. When they emigrated to non-white countries, it was mainly into positions of power as soldiers, priests, teachers, doctors, landowning settlers and businesspeople – all based on their economic and social clout as white people. Not to mention the role Irishmen played in the day-to-day administration and management of the British Empire which provided job opportunities before and after independence.

Even if they arrived empty-handed, they had more than the oppressed indigenous population because of the colour of their skin. An aunt and uncle of mine who worked in a hotel bar in South Africa in the early 1970s at the height of apartheid were automatically given more responsibility and respect than their black colleagues enjoyed.

When the Irish emigrated to white-majority countries, principally the United States, Britain and Australia, there were many challenges but race was not one of them. This simple truth has not prevented the advent of 'whiteness studies' which claim the Irish did not 'become white' in the US until the middle of the 20th century.

Historically, in the three countries mentioned, the Irish who emigrated (assuming they had no money and were uneducated, which most were) started at the bottom of the social ladder, particularly when it still mattered which Christian denomination you belonged to. They joined a society dominated in the case of the US by a Protestant Anglo-Saxon and Germanic establishment and faced significant discrimination and hostility, just like other European nationalities and ethnic groups – such as Italian, Polish, Greek and Jewish immigrants – did. It was not until after the First World War that these delineations began to fade and it started to matter less if the older white ethnicities of the US thought various other groups were inferior to them. But even with these prejudices in place, the Irish were white and as such could always enjoy the benefits of the dominant race. No Irish were segregated, legally barred from attending white-only schools or refused entry to certain professions or unions. They were not denied the vote as citizens or prosecuted for marrying a white person. The Irish were never completely barred from entering the country, as the Chinese were by the Chinese Exclusion Act from 1882 to 1943. With their numbers, their networks and the better economic opportunities open to whites, the Irish were destined to rise through the ranks, given enough time, whether high society liked it or not.

Some 37.4 million Americans claim Irish ancestry, according to the last census (2010). By the time my first cousins started emigrating to the US in the 1980s, Irish emigrants had no shortage of powerful friends in Washington. Two visa programmes – Donnelly and Morrison, both spearheaded by Irish-American politicians – were disproportionately generous to Irish applicants,

St Patrick's Day, 2017: Mike Pence, Paul Ryan, Donald Trump, the Irish Taoiseach Enda Kenny and congressman Peter King after a 'Friends of Ireland' lunch at the Capitol Building in Washington.

and managed to regularise the bulk of the undocumented Irish. Created in 1987, Brian J. Donnelly's Diversity Visa Program was awarded on a first-come, first-served basis, through which the Irish, who were well-organised, won 40 per cent of the visas over a four-year period. Under the subsequent Morrison scheme, some 48,000 Irish were legalised between 1991 and 1994.

Bruce Morrison was inducted into the 'Irish Hall of Fame', an honour bestowed by *Irish America* magazine since 2010. This has become a who's who of Irish-American success which shows how firmly the Irish occupy positions of power and prestige in modern America. The four 2018 inductees give a flavour of this record of distinction – Governor Jerry Brown of California; former CIA director John Brennan; actor, singer and Tony Award-winner Kelli O'Hara; and Dennis Long, former president of Anheuser-Busch.

The Irish slave meme

The claims of victimisation have resurfaced in more recent years on social media with the Irish slave meme, a sinister ploy intended to negate concerns about present-day racial discrimination in the United States. Variations of the Irish slave meme continue to circulate online garnering millions of likes and views. Whether or not the interest is based on innocent curiosity or eagerness to belittle African Americans is revealed by the comments.

The tone of these memes varies from innocuous, allowing you to draw the racist dots (or not) yourself, to downright insulting and aggressive, depending on the audience passing it along. For example, the quote below appeared as the caption on a 1911 photo of child labourers from a Pennsylvania coalmine. This photo and caption was posted on a Facebook group called 'Irish Americans' and got almost 600,000 shares:

'White Irish slaves were treated worse than any other race in the US. When was the last time you heard an Irishman bitching that the world owes him a living?'

Limerick historian Liam Hogan has devoted six years to debunking the slave myth, having correctly identified that it is being exploited by the white nationalist movement to dismiss the unique significance of black chattel slavery in American history.

Hogan's efforts are paying off, with minor publications retracting inaccurate articles and large media outlets covering the story. An open letter, signed by 82 Irish scholars around the world, denounced the slave myth in 2016.

For the record, the Irish in the United States were never slaves. Slaveowners in many cases, but not slaves. A poor labourer is not the same as a slave whose children are sold at auction. A poor labourer gets paid and can leave town, marry, change jobs, maybe even prosper one day.

A fresh start

No matter how many times you see these famine numbers, it's staggering. The population of the territory now in the Republic of Ireland fell like a stone from the time of the famine, declining from a high of six and a half million in 1841 to just below three million in the 1920s, the first decade of independence. The numbers continued to stagnate or decline for the middle years of the century, and did not get up above three million again until the 1970s. Apart from a wobble in the 1980s, Irish population growth has been strong since then, 'a combination of natural increase and declining net outward migration', according to the CSO, 'resulting in the current population being almost 70 per cent larger than in 1961'.

It is not just about being pushed into leaving. Pull factors have always been a significant aspect of Irish emigration, and any migration. Those who go ahead and become established may paint an appealing picture of the good life they have now. They are able to sponsor family members, organise paperwork, pay their passage and find them a place to stay and work, so-called chain migration. The old emigrants become a pull factor. My grandmother's siblings all emigrated to the United States one after the other in this way, leaving her alone to inherit the family farm, on the one hand making room, on the other hand depriving their community of the immeasurable contribution they could have made, if the conditions had been different.

There were other reasons for leaving, apart from economic. The oppressive moral codes enforced by the Catholic Church and the majority Catholic population were unbearable for some, especially victims of the Magdalene laundries (or those at risk of being incarcerated) and children's institutions but also anyone not prepared to live a conventional life. England, within easy reach, became a convenient place for Irish people to disappear and start again, the slate wiped clean of prejudice. Others were bored by Ireland with its censorship and prudery, the valley of the squinting windows atmosphere.

Those are reasons people left Ireland in the past but what about now when Ireland is progressive and relatively prosperous? The majority of Irish emigrants today are young and well-educated, seeking better opportunities and earning potential along with some adventure. The figures fluctuate but the traffic is two-way. We are now back in positive territory with more Irish nationals returning to Ireland than leaving. Going back to the most recent recession, in the six-year period 2008 to 2014, an estimated 228,000 Irish nationals emigrated while 108,000 Irish migrants returned, leaving a net departure figure of 120,000 Irish nationals, according to the Nevin Economic Research Institute (Neri).

Writing in 2015, Tom Healy of Neri noted: 'As in previous Irish recessions, outward migration has acted as a very significant 'safety valve' in facilitating the movement of a large number of young persons to other countries to take up work there.'

The then finance minister, Michael Noonan, caused a furore in 2012 when he described emigration as a free lifestyle choice rather than a necessity. That was just a few weeks before youth unemployment reached an all-time high of 31.6 per cent, more than twice the national level of 14.8 per cent. Doors were closing everywhere for entry-level workers: this period also saw a recruitment and promotion moratorium in public service jobs from 2009.

For a close-up of who emigrated in recent times and to test Noonan's claim, University College Cork's Emigre project[iv] provides excellent data on the period 2006 to 2013. Emigrants were young (70 per cent in their twenties), more highly educated than the average population, and most were not leaving directly because of unemployment. While one in four were unemployed, almost half were in full-time employment and 15 per cent were students or recent graduates. Some 28 per cent had previous experience of living abroad. The most popular destinations were the UK and Australia and, on average, emigrants rated their quality of life abroad as much better than in Ireland.

This is economic migration but the experience is more tinged with privilege than desperation. Apart from needing destination countries that are open to your nationality, you need funds to emigrate, preferably third-level education or good training, confidence, and in many cases connections. The UCC survey found that 55 per cent of emigrants had friends or family already living at their destination. Contemporary Irish emigrants belong to a dynamic, outward-looking segment of the population. Some Irish people do not tick these boxes and never will. They do not therefore have the wherewithal to emigrate.

Another striking feature of contemporary emigrants is how connected they remain to their home community through social media, as well as being connected with other Irish abroad. One woman in her twenties interviewed by the Emigre project was working as an architect in London. She described how her interaction with friends by WhatsApp makes her feel closer and more related to them.

'[M]y group of friends have a WhatsApp conversation that goes on between seven or eight of us constantly. So there's someone in China, there's two of us here in London, there's people in Australia and in Canada and in Ireland.'

But however close they may stay to their previous life, Irish citizens abroad soon lose their political voice. They only retain the right to vote for 18 months after moving abroad, as long as they intend to come back to Ireland. As there is no postal vote, this means returning in person to vote, as many did in recent referendums in a celebratory mood captured by the 'hometovote' hashtag.

The economic picture has changed dramatically since the period examined in the Emigre survey, to the extent that people who may have settled overseas in those years are now being courted to return to Ireland to work. One Irish recruitment company, FRS Recruitment, staged a roadshow in Australia in November 2018 called Ireland is Hiring. They were offering free flights in an attempt to convince Irish people to come back to fill job vacancies at home.

'Ireland currently has 12,000 IT job vacancies, more than 2,500 jobs in MedTech firms, 2,300 jobs in the agri-food sector, 150 vacancies for doctors, 100 other healthcare sector jobs, and 120 professional posts in construction, and large numbers of financial sector vacancies,' Colin Donnery, general manager of the company boasted.

You can't help wondering when the wheel will turn again.

New Ireland

We know the story of *Brooklyn*. But as much as Ireland is a country of emigrants, it is also now a country of immigrants. One of the most successful Irish films of all time was Oscar-winning *Once*, the heart-warming story of an Irish busker and a Czech immigrant in Dublin falling in love through music. This 2007 film showing a young Eastern-European woman in precarious circumstances trying to get established in Ireland was very close to reality.

Eastern Europeans are heavily represented among the new Irish. The top ten foreign nationalities in Ireland as recorded in the 2016 census are:

1. Polish (122,515)
2. British (103,113)
3. Lithuanian (36,552)
4. Romanian (29,196)
5. Latvian (19,933)
6. Brazilian (13,640)
7. Spanish (12,112)
8. Italian (11,732)
9. French (11,661)
10. German (11,531).

We also have an indigenous ethnic minority, recognised as such by the State in 2017: Irish Travellers, who number some 30,000.

Changes on the ground are extraordinary in some places. Ballyjamesduff, 100 kilometres from Dublin in the border county of Cavan, is a small town immortalised in Percy French's 1912 song of emigration, *Come Back Paddy Reilly to Ballyjamesduff*. Yet the latest census figures show that Ballyjamesduff has the fourth highest immigrant population of all Irish towns, with 30 per cent of its population of 2,869 made up of non-Irish nationals. Newcomers have been attracted by jobs – many in the local meat plant and in mushroom farms – as well as affordable housing and a good quality of life.

The changes can be seen most dramatically in the local secondary school, which has doubled its enrolment in 15 years and now has pupils of 29 nationalities. On a visit to St. Clare's College, I met a very diverse Transition Year class. Around half were long-term locals, the rest had moved to the Cavan town from Dublin or from overseas. The countries of origin of the students included Poland, Croatia, Botswana, Nigeria, Lithuania and China. The principal Teresa Donnellan remembers the first non-Irish student who joined the school in the late 1990s, a Polish boy. Now there are more than 300 Polish people living in the town, enough to keep a Polish grocery shop going.

Most immigrants to Ireland – some 60 per cent – have third level education. They are at the beginning or in the middle of their working life. They are by definition looking for work, attracted by the economic opportunities. The vast majority end up as net financial contributors to the economy. Most are EU citizens, especially since the EU enlarged by ten new members in 2004. In terms of how the newcomers are faring, a 2018 ESRI report monitoring the integration of immigrants found that non-Irish nationals were matching Irish nationals on several key economic and social indicators, but that some groups remained disadvantaged[v].

'In 2016, some 23 per cent of non-Irish nationals were living below the income poverty line (drawn at 60 per cent of median household income) compared to just under 16 per cent of Irish nationals. Consistent poverty rates (the proportion of a group that is income poor and experiencing basic deprivation) were 13 per cent for non-Irish as a whole, compared to 8 per cent for Irish. This rate was very high for non-EU nationals (29 per cent),' the report read.

The Irish Census has only included a question on nationality since 2002. That year, 5.8 per cent of the population recorded a nationality other than Irish. The rate had increased to 10.1 per cent by 2006, at the height of the Celtic Tiger boom. The proportion of non-nationals rose to 12.2 per cent in 2011, falling back a little since then to reach 11.6 per cent in the 2016 census. That still puts Ireland well above the EU average of 7.5 per cent.

That the percentage of immigrants is falling is partly due to immigrants going through the naturalisation process, after which they are counted as Irish. Citizenship comes at a price – a €175 application fee and €950 for the cert. Successful applicants, who must have lived for five years in Ireland, are required to attend a citizenship ceremony in which they make a declaration of fidelity to the nation.

On November 26, 2018, Taoiseach Leo Varadkar tweeted a photo of the crowd at the citizenship ceremony:

'Killarney today: 3,000 new citizens sworn in. Since 2011, about 120,000 people have become Irish citizens, strengthening our economy, running our public services and enriching our society. Congratulations.'

Official Ireland currently welcomes immigrants, that much is clear and contrasts with the language used by political leaders next door in the UK. Efforts to set up political movements with an anti-immigration, nativist platform, such as Renua in 2015 ('putting Ireland's interests and people first') and Irexit Freedom Party in 2018 ('taking back control by the Irish people of ... our borders and immigration policy') have produced feeble results, indicating that there is no great appetite for this style of politics in Ireland.

In terms of visibility of the new Irish in public life, we have a Taoiseach who is the son of an Indian immigrant. Even his harshest critics draw no attention to his ethnic or second-generation immigrant background because there is no political capital to be gained by demonstrating xenophobia. His cabinet includes an American-born minister, Katherine Zappone. The weather report on public radio is regularly read by meteorologists with foreign accents. But these are exceptions that do not change the fact that the people who run, inform and entertain the country are still almost exclusively Irish without a migration background. However, Irish people with a migration background are inevitably coming through the system. Journalist Zainab Boladale from Ennis, County Clare, who was hired by RTÉ in 2017, is the national broadcaster's first news anchor of Afro-Irish heritage.

Irish residents aged over 18 of any nationality are eligible to vote in local elections for city and county councils. They also have the right to stand in local elections. Only 9 of Ireland's 949 councillors have a migrant background so there is definitely room for local politics to become more representative and provide an avenue to integration and agency. The May 2019 local elections saw Ireland's first black woman elected, Yemi Adenuga from Nigeria, as well as two Muslim men. Adenuga, a first-time candidate for Fine Gael and a reality television show participant (*Gogglebox Ireland*), got a seat on Meath County Council. Bangladeshi-born Kazi Ahmed was elected to Dun Laoghaire-Rathdown County Council and Abul Kalam Azad Talukder took a seat for Fianna Fáil in Limerick. In Dublin's Pembroke Ward, Hazel Chu, an Irish citizen and second-generation immigrant whose parents moved to Ireland from Hong Kong in the 1970s, became the first Chinese-Irish person to be elected to public office.

On the edge

Always at the bottom of the immigration ladder, asylum seekers make up a fluctuating share of immigrants (currently below five per cent) and bear the brunt of any anti-immigrant or racist prejudice. Some 5,000 people are living in 34 direct provision centres around Ireland as part of a system in place since 2000. The centres include former hostels, hotels and a mobile home park. Residents, who receive only pocket money, are not allowed to leave the centres overnight.

Reports of arbitrary cruelty by staff at the privately-run centres, such as denying a snack for a sick child, are having an impact on public opinion. The connection is being made in people's minds with historical state injustice involving the detention of vulnerable groups such as unmarried mothers and their children.

'To bear a system of enforced dependency, strict meal times, shared accommodation with strangers for six months would be difficult, to do so for any period of time beyond this is cruel and inhuman,' Dr Liam Thornton of the UCD School of Law wrote in an opinion piece in the *Irish Independent* [vi].

On the positive side, asylum seekers are finally allowed to work, under certain conditions, following a Supreme Court case that ruled in 2017 that the ban on working was unconstitutional. It took more than a year for the government to introduce measures to make this possible, measures which were soon overtaken by new EU rules. Now, applicants who have been in Ireland for nine months or more and have not had a first decision made on their refugee status have the right to work in any job without a fee or restrictions which were in place before. This is estimated to apply to 3,000 people.

Over the past 5 years, the annual number of asylum applicants has ranged from 1,448 to 3,726. There was a rapid increase in asylum numbers in the 1990s, reaching more than 11,000 in 2002. That sparked debate about the lure of the 'Irish baby', the phenomenon of foreign parents who were undocumented or who had their asylum applications rejected but subsequently gained the right to remain based on their child's Irish nationality through birth (ie, the child was born in Ireland).

Ireland has traditionally had a combination of two principles of granting citizenship – by soil, *jus soli*, and by blood, *jus sanguinis*. It is still the case that all children born of Irish parents have automatic citizenship. There is also a restricted version of that for grandchildren of Irish citizens, currently being widely used by

British nationals of Irish origin keen to hold onto EU citizenship post Brexit.

But in a 2004 referendum, Irish voters removed the automatic entitlement to birthright citizenship, based on a perception that this right was acting as a magnet for undocumented pregnant women to come to the country to give birth. The law then changed to specify that non-national parents of Irish-born children had to prove they had a genuine link to Ireland before their child would be entitled to Irish citizenship, evidenced by having lived three of the four years before the birth in Ireland.

The debate went away but the new rules inevitably created hardship cases of children born in Ireland, whose parents' status was uncertain, having no access to Irish nationality despite never having lived anywhere else. The threatened deportation of an Irish-born boy from Bray, Co Wicklow of Chinese parents placed the issue back on the agenda, and moves are under way for a proposed reform of the law brought by the Labour Party. In the meantime, renewed attention to the issue makes it likely that the Department of Justice will use its discretion to act humanely in the small number of cases where this crops up.

An accidental emigrant

Before leaving the topic of emigration, I cannot omit my own experience as someone who has lived two thirds of my life in Ireland and one third abroad. What kind of emigrant am I? An accidental one, I would say. There was certainly no master plan. Unemployment was still high when I graduated from university in 1995 and I would have been a prime candidate for emigration then. Working in a low-paid job with no security and no clear prospects, I could have done what my former classmates were doing and looked for opportunities in London, Paris and Moscow.

As it happened, I wasn't done with Dublin and Dublin wasn't done with me. Though we didn't know it, there was an economic boom around the corner and, after four years of casual work in various places, I landed my first contract in *The Irish Times* in 2000.

In the end, I emigrated for love after I met a Swiss man. I was still young enough to think I was just trying out a new country, that this would be temporary just like everything else in my life was temporary. Marriage and children changed that state of affairs.

For me, being an emigrant is an ongoing and often taxing condition. I have to practice gratitude and acceptance to work around the losses and gains. Though I'm doing well in Switzerland, I have an Ireland-shaped hole in my heart that no amount of return visits can fill. It turns out, as many emigrants find, leaving Ireland when you are young is easier than returning when you're older. Not just because of the ties of the new country but also in the sense that you never step into the same river twice. The Ireland I lived in is no longer there however hard I try to recapture it; many returned emigrants can attest to that. Mary Robinson's candle in the window wasn't meant for the likes of me but I too have to resist the pull of self-pity. When I left by ferry last summer after a long stay, pulling out of Cork Harbour in the dusk, I would have made a good extra for *Brooklyn* with my sad face looking back on the country I was about to lose forever, or for a few months anyway.

In focus: Designing a new life in Ireland

Father-of-two Piotr Mach came to Ireland in September 2007 right after qualifying as an architect in his hometown of Gliwice, Poland. He and his wife Karolina, also an architect, had dreamt of living in Ireland, and when they saw an ad for jobs in Limerick, posted by a returned Polish emigrant on a notice board at their university, they felt it was meant to be.

'Our first big dreams were going to come true! The plan was to move to Ireland for around two years to gain some experience, save some money and come back home, as most of the Poles were doing those days.

Ireland was offering and still offers huge possibilities to those who want to take it. Only your abilities count first and foremost here. Polish people living in Ireland have a very good reputation. They are considered to be hardworking, reliable and doing very well in different situations, regardless of their profession.

My wife and I fell deeply in love with Ireland and Irish hospitality! Even when the crisis hit in 2008 and we lost our jobs, we still believed that it was the place for us. It was hard to get a regular job so we started working as consultants and freelance 3D modellers, mostly designing small house extensions and creating computerised visualisations. We believed that the downturn would end soon. As we know now, it lasted for a good few years and the whole building industry completely collapsed. Things started to improve slowly in 2012 when I got a full-time job in my profession. My first child was also born that year. That was like a breath of fresh air for us after a very unstable and unpredictable four years.

I never felt like a foreigner here. Irish people are so nice and open, and if you need a hand, they will help you in whatever way they can. They smile a lot and apologise countless times a day. Irish people are what I love most about Ireland and what makes other Poles want to stay longer here.'

Piotr currently works for an architectural firm in Limerick and teaches at the Polish Saturday School in the city. His projects have been nominated for a number of architectural and industry awards.

Endnotes

[i] *Ireland 1912–1985: Politics and Society*, J.J. Lee, p. 374

[ii] 'Irish Emigration Patterns and Citizens Abroad,' Department of Foreign Affairs and Trade, Irish Abroad Unit, 20.06.2017

[iii] Illustration from Preface to the First Edition of *An Illustrated History of Ireland from AD 400 to 1800*, by Mary Frances Cusack, illustrated by Henry Doyle.

[iv] Current Irish EMIGration and REturn (Emigre for short), a 12-month project carried out by the Department of Geography and Institute for Social Science, University College Cork.

[v] 'Monitoring Report on Integration 2018', 07.11.2018

[vi] Comment: 'It's time to move away from direct provision', *Irish Independent*, 01.01.2018

CHAPTER 2

The Irish are Violent

The struggle is brief. He is thrown down in the dirt, their knees sharp on his back and arms. Though he is winded, he stays calm. In the black pool below, he sees the golden glow of the rising sun on the water. A beautiful day in store. What is the sense of it?

When they are done with him, he knows his body will be staked to the bottom of that pool, his guts spilled open and his head cut off. Almost gently, they roll him over and paint the sign on his bare chest. At the first strike he manages to free his arm and stop the blade. At the second strike he is helpless and he gives himself to the pain.

This is an imagined account of the last moments of Old Croghan Man, one of Ireland's earliest known murder victims, whose preserved torso was found in a County Offaly bog in 2003. This man from the Iron Age (550 BC – 400 AD) was part of a tragic brotherhood, along with Derrycashel Man, Gallagh Man, Clonycavan Man and, the oldest of all, Cashel man from County Laois.

These were young men whose remains, preserved in the oxygen-free, acidic conditions of the peat bogs, date back 2,000 to 4,000 years ago. They were all violently murdered in their prime in what may have been ritual killings.

Where there is humankind, there is violence. And in Northern Europe, where there are bogs, there are bog bodies. Hundreds of bodies, mainly from the Iron Age, have been found in Denmark, Germany, the Netherlands, Britain and Ireland, indicating a common practice of killing outcasts and burying them in particular places with a particular meaning for the people.

A lot has happened since Old Croghan Man met his grisly end. Empires have risen and fallen. Ireland has been a theatre of invasion for Vikings, Normans and the English. The Irish were too fragmented and regionalised a society and too busy defending themselves to ever seek to expand their territory overseas. Most of Irish history is a catalogue of lost battles and failed rebellions on home ground, a nation condemned to fight back.

Are we still fighting? Some people seem to think so. Whether we like it or not, and unless we are professional fighters capitalising on the association as part of our brand, we generally don't like it, the Irish have a reputation for violence. As recently as March 2019, at a White House event celebrating Irish heritage, the President of the United States was inspired to remark:

'They are brutal enemies, right? So you have to keep them as your friend. Always keep them as your friend. You don't want to fight with the Irish. It's too tough, too bloody.'[i]

Obviously it's a clumsy, unoriginal attempt at humour, but the stereotype to which Donald Trump was referring is familiar to all Americans, and has been for generations. It bears little relation to Irish society today but it persists nonetheless.

Despite the recent spate of drug-related gangland killings, Ireland is in line with the global trend of decreasing violent crime in developed countries. The murder rate is low, below 1 per 100,000 people, as is the incarceration rate, by international standards (82 per 100,000, compared to 716 in the US and 148 in England and Wales). There is no death penalty in neutral Ireland and the small Irish army is only deployed on peacekeeping missions. As for policing, the national police force, An Garda Síochána (guardian of the peace), is predominantly unarmed and the killing of unarmed civilians by police is virtually unknown. So where does the violent reputation come from?

Ruffians

Some of the prejudice has its origins in the period of mass migration of Irish to America in the 19th century and the social impact of that influx of often traumatised people. In an article based on his trip to the US, Charles Dickens described the Irish slums of eastern cities as 'pandemoniums of strife and quarrelling'. His depiction of the lawless Irish is laced with class prejudice and would have struck a chord with his readers in Victorian Britain at a time when one in 20 London residents was Irish.

'It is hard to conceive a more abandoned ruffian than the downright bad Irishman. The same spirit which commits agrarian crime on the soil of Erin, survives the Atlantic voyage, crops out on the other side, and fills the American courts and prisons with criminals of a most desperate and incorrigible class.'[ii]

The agrarian violence referred to by Dickens was carried out by the secret societies that sprang up in rural Ireland in the 18th and 19th centuries. This happened in the context of the penal laws and in response to the injustices of the hated landlord system. The different societies had many names – the Terry Alts, Molly Maguires, Hearts of Steel Boys, the Black Feet and more – but can be grouped together as the Whiteboy movement after the name of the first such organisation, active in Munster from the 1760s. This description is from author and former US ambassador to Ireland (1977 – 1981), William V. Shannon:

'These groups had no political programs or large aims. They

took action on specific local grievances. If a landlord converted tilled fields into grazing lands, the Whiteboys maimed his cattle or burned his outbuildings. If a landlord expelled a tenant for failing to meet the rent, few dared to take the farm in his stead, for fear of retaliation from the neighbours.'[iii]

The underground violence also included killings, beatings and house raids. In parallel, troublemakers faced hanging or transportation and poverty-stricken tenants were evicted or had their houses destroyed. It was an undeclared war between big landowners, backed by the forces of law and order, and the subsistence farmers living on the land. There was, as always, a wider economic context: the high demand for meat in the English market. The landowners wanted to consolidate smallholdings into larger, more economic divisions and to clear 'excess people' to make way for cattle. That was where the money was.

The system created such abject misery that it could not be maintained without violence or the threat of violence. To the landowners and the colonial administration, the violence they carried out to protect their property and income was justified. It was only the violence they experienced in response that was worth condemning and would be heard about by concerned citizens like Dickens in England. And this is partly how the inconvenient Irish poor of this era came to be defined as violent by nature.

Putting the bomb into politics

But it is not just crime and public order that were portrayed as an Irish problem. The Irish reputation for violence has been kept alive, above all, by political violence in the 19th and 20th centuries.

After the Great Famine, a new generation of Irish nationalists became radicalised, embracing the idea that the best course of action was to end British rule through armed insurrection, a project last attempted in a concerted way in 1798 by the United Irishmen with sorry results.

These revolutionaries adopted the name of Fenians, after the Fianna warriors of Irish mythology, and were active on both sides of the Atlantic Ocean. Two sister organisations, the Irish Republican Brotherhood and its American counterpart the Fenian Brotherhood, were founded in 1858. While they operated in secret in Ireland, the Fenians were tolerated in the US and openly organised and raised funds for the cause of Irish freedom there. They went as far as assembling a small army and staging an invasion of the British Province of Canada in 1866 from the US side of the border, three years before Dickens' visit.

Despite winning the first battle, the Irish were soon dispersed by US forces. The Fenian plans to provoke a war between the US and the UK, exploiting the tense relations between the countries, or to capture Canada and swap it for Ireland came to nothing.

Another Fenian tactic was to bomb British targets on British soil. They carried out bombings across Britain, mainly in the 1880s, and assassinated top officials in Dublin. These actions provided fodder for British and American cartoonists of the day who depicted the Irish as dangerous, and often apish, thugs.

The Irishman as terrorist or freedom fighter kept his role in the 20th century, both in real life and in film. He was a staple in the canon of Irish-themed cinema financed abroad, mostly governed by a mythology 'sustained and perpetuated' by the Irish diaspora, as film studies professor Marcia Landy explained.

'In particular, Hollywood and British cinema exploited Irishness, offering a screen mythology of the fighting Irish, the bloodthirsty Irish Republican Army (IRA), and the garrulous, ineffectual, often alcoholic but charming Irishman.'[iv]

These figures were all versions of the Stage Irishman, a

PUNCH, OR THE LONDON CHARIVARI.—December 28, 1867.

THE FENIAN GUY FAWKES.

Punch cartoon in December 1867 by John Tenniel following the Clerkenwell explosion, carried out by the Fenians, that killed 12 people in London that month. The woman and children represent the victims.

throwback from 19th-century theatre. Various incarnations appear in John Ford's *The Quiet Man* (1952), a positive cornucopia of Irish stereotypes, which also gave us the wild, irrational Irish woman in need of taming.

The Quiet Man was sacrosanct in my childhood because my deceased grandfather, Joseph O'Dea, had a small role in the film as the train guard. Whenever the film was shown on television, we all gathered in my grandmother's room upstairs to watch Joe's few lines of dialogue. In one scene, he gives confusing Oirish directions to John Wayne who is trying to get to Inisfree. John Wayne's character, Sean Thornton, is returning to his birthplace after a career as a boxer (what else?) in the States.

The climactic fight scene in *The Quiet Man* lasts for about nine minutes, including a break in the pub. The fight is between Sean Thornton and the boorish Will Danaher (Victor McLaglen), brother of Thornton's fiery, red-headed fiancée Kate Danaher (Maureen O'Hara).

The people of Inisfree follow the fight all around the locality, occasionally joining in. Everyone is having the time of their lives and indeed one man gets up from his deathbed when he hears the commotion. John Ford, whose parents were born in County Galway, was reaching for a romanticised version of rural Ireland, a purer, simpler version of the country that fits the immigrant fantasy.

Troubled times

But all trace of romanticism was gone in the Ireland of the 1970s, 1980s and 1990s. I once worked in a business owned by a former IRA prisoner. Several other members of staff had connections to the IRA. One day at work, we heard the news that a nun had been killed in a roadside bomb near Armagh. She was driving past at the same moment as the bomb's intended target, a police patrol car. Her name was Catherine Dunne and she was 37. Three men, an RUC constable and two reserve officers, also in their thirties, were killed too.

The response from my colleagues was little more than a shrug as they trotted out the phrase: 'Every armed conflict has civilian casualties'. They were not going to waste emotion on a small mistake like that, and certainly not spare a thought for the three 'legitimate targets' who had been killed.

A young woman called Cathy McCann was in the car with Sister Catherine that day in 1990. She almost lost her life too but by some miracle she survived her serious injuries. It was not the first time that Cathy's family had been touched by deadly violence. Her father, John Gallagher, was one of the first victims of the conflict. He was shot dead by the B-Specials (a discredited quasi-military force, the Ulster Special Constabulary, which was disbanded in 1970) in street disturbances in Armagh in 1969 when she was a young child. Another John Gallagher, no relation, was killed in an Ulster Volunteer Force bombing of a pub in Belfast in 1974[v]. I could go on. 'Every armed conflict has civilian casualties.'

The violence that is seared into the national consciousness and brought us infamy abroad for many years *is* this political and sectarian violence. In the last three decades of the last century, no other location in the wider European region experienced such an intensity of terrorist violence as Northern Ireland during the Troubles (1969-1998).

The violence mostly happened in Ireland but it is not purely Irish violence. Apart from the infamous IRA and lesser remembered Irish National Liberation Army (INLA) who killed and maimed people with the supposed goal of ending British rule in Northern Ireland, there was the terrifying spectre of the Ulster Volunteer Force (UVF) and Ulster Defence Association / Ulster Freedom Fighters (UDA/UFF) paramilitary violence. The latter groups sometimes targeted IRA members but mostly any Catholic civilian would do. A significant number of these loyalist killings were facilitated or directed by British security forces, collusion that took place with total impunity. And, bringing up the rear in terms of numbers of victims, there was the violence carried out by the British Army and Northern Irish security forces.

The statistics show that republican paramilitaries were responsible for the most deaths. Catholic civilians were the group who suffered the most losses. The dead included some 1,200 Catholic civilians and some 700 Protestant civilians.

Deaths related to the Troubles, 1969 – 2001	
Organisation	Count
British Security	363
Irish Security	5
Loyalist Paramilitary	1027
Unknown	80
Republican Paramilitary	2057
TOTAL	**3532**

Source: The Sutton Index of Deaths

Like most people living in the Republic of Ireland and Northern Ireland in those years, I abhorred the violence that formed the news backdrop to my life and hung like a dead weight over politics and society. But the impact in my part of the country, Dublin, was nebulous. I was too young to remember the Dublin and Monaghan UVF bombings of 1974 that caused the worst single day in terms of loss of life of the Troubles. In my memory, the death and destruction were always happening a safe distance away. The closest I got to the pain was reading out the names of the victims of the Omagh bombing as a radio newsreader. So I give the floor to Belfast journalists who had to cover the bombings and shootings and look survivors in the eye.

By the time the peace agreement came in 1998, there was no comprehensive record of all those who had been killed in the Troubles. But there was one under way. Four Belfast journalists – David McKittrick, Seamus Kelters, Brian Feeney and Chris

Thornton – had taken on the task of recording the lives of those killed. They began with the intention of compiling a list but the list grew to a description of each person killed and the circumstances, including the many connections between the different deaths. The book, *Lost Lives: The stories of the men, women and children who died as the result of the Northern Ireland troubles,* was published by Mainstream in 1999.

Writing in the *Independent* newspaper, David McKittrick described some of the heart-rending testimonies the authors collected.

'There are hundreds more stories like these of terrible deaths and terrible injuries, of shattered lives and shattered families, of widows and orphans whose suffering will go on. It has taken us eight years, and almost a million words, to attempt to do justice to all this. ...

Those who have died in the Troubles include civilians; members of loyalist and republican groups; political figures; soldiers; joyriders; alleged drug dealers; judges and magistrates; prison officers; police officers; convicted killers; businessmen; alleged informers; hunger strikers; men; women; children; pensioners and unborn babies.'[vi]

When your life is not marked by violence, it is easy to condemn and distance yourself from an atrocity. At the end of the day it isn't personal. Looking back at those young men I worked with who had developed an indifference to violence, I have to acknowledge the huge contrast in our circumstances. I was middle-class, a university student from a leafy part of Dun Laoghaire, the product of a secure and happy childhood. They were disenfranchised, working class, Northern Irish children of the 1970s and 1980s for whom violence was all-pervasive and normalised. They were treated as the enemy by the forces of the state from a young age.

Growing up in a war-torn city, 'in those dark days, which were the extreme of days' as Anna Burns writes in *Milkman* (winner of the 2018 Man Booker Prize), they suffered a lot and came to think it was all right for others to suffer too.

Then and now

The other problem for 'Southerners' like me is that whenever debates arose about the legitimacy of political violence in Ireland, there was the uncomfortable reality that my country would not exist if people had not once been prepared to resort to arms without much of a mandate.

As the season of centenaries of the struggle for Irish independence progresses, we are vividly reminded of the difficult birth of this nation that involved an unsuccessful insurrection, a war of independence and a civil war, all of which cost lives.

But that is not to say that resorting to violence is the default Irish modus operandi because, historically, Irish efforts to change British rule in any way involved long periods of attempting to secure greater self-determination through peaceful means. That was the pattern, from the United Irishmen to the campaign for Home Rule to the civil rights movement in the North. Those efforts were rebuffed and progress denied for so long until the peaceful path was deemed futile by some.

On a governmental level, Irish leaders have always been in this difficult position of allowing the violence of the independence struggle to be glorified while violence linked to that tradition continued in a way the Republic did not want to be seen to condone. The two most powerful political parties today, Fianna Fáil and Fine Gael, are the contemporary incarnations of groupings that fought on opposite sides in the Civil War one hundred years ago – (Old) Sinn Féin and Cumann na nGaedheal respectively. Traditionally, the old enemies have walked a different line on this, as historian Conor Kostick explained to me:

'Fianna Fáil were historically fairly comfortable with the narrative of the noble generation who sacrificed themselves for the nation because they were the political descendants and sometimes physical descendants of that generation. But I think there was always an argument in Fine Gael which derives from John Redmond's [Home Rule] politics that these were radical troublemakers who went about things the wrong way, and so a section of the Irish state and establishment was prepared to re-examine the recent past in a more unsympathetic way, giving us revisionism.'

In the context of the indiscriminate killing of civilians, all mainstream Irish political parties have distanced themselves completely from the modern IRA. This position was reinforced by the revisionist approach to history in Irish academia which became ingrained from the 1960s. Its agenda was to destroy the sacred cows of Irish nationalism and to challenge the simplistic narrative of heroic resistance and epic suffering, for example by minimising the tragedy and significance of the Famine or by pouring scorn on the participants in the 1916 Rising. The revisionist line was never widely accepted by the general population who were content to honour the rebels while rejecting modern-day violence. Since the peace process at the end of the last century, Irish revisionism has lost its grip, and it has been possible to develop a more nuanced interpretation of history which is not trying too hard to prove either case.

Gangland

Around the time guns were becoming less relevant in Northern Ireland, there was an upsurge in organised crime in Dublin.

One of the most shocking crimes of the 1990s was the murder of 37-year-old journalist Veronica Guerin. A renowned crime reporter with the *Sunday Independent*, she was shot in her car on a weekday afternoon as she waited at traffic lights in the outskirts of Dublin. Two men on a motorbike pulled up alongside her and the pillion passenger fired a hail of bullets into the car. An outrageous crime on what should have been an ordinary summer's afternoon, Wednesday, June 26 1996.

Guerin had become a minor celebrity for her work exposing nefarious figures in the Irish criminal underworld, work which made her powerful enemies. Her most dangerous enemy was crime boss John Gilligan, later convicted of drug-smuggling but cleared of her murder. At the time of the murder, Gilligan was living in a seven-bedroom house on an 80-acre estate which included Jessbrook equestrian centre in Kildare.

Guerin's funeral was broadcast live and the scenes of her seven-year-old boy Cathal in attendance touched the nation's heart. The

Veronica Guerin's widower Graham Turley and son Cathal Turley at her funeral in 1996.

drug lords were now out of hand and the government had carte blanche to act decisively against them. Within months, the Dáil had introduced legislation to set up the Criminal Assets Bureau which allowed law enforcement authorities to confiscate the proceeds of crime. The onus is on the suspected criminal to prove their assets or income came from a legitimate source. After a 20-year court battle by Gilligan, mostly fought from behind bars, the last portion of Jessbrook, along with the house, was sold by the Criminal Assets Bureau in 2018.[vii]

Gilligan was one of many names introduced to the public by Veronica Guerin and other crime journalists in the 1990s. A close associate of Gilligan's, Brian Meehan, was convicted of the journalist's murder in 1999 and sentenced to life imprisonment. The case against Meehan was partly based on one of the co-conspirators, Charles Bowden, turning State's witness. He was the first person ever to enter the State's witness protection programme. Another lynchpin of the gang, John Traynor, was never convicted in Ireland but served time in the UK for fraud.

These figures have passed out of the public eye now but a new generation has taken their place and Ireland still has a gun crime problem both in terms of a high demand for illicit firearms and a high rate of homicide by shooting. Twenty years after Guerin's death, another landmark killing took place in Dublin that shocked the country.

Two men dressed as elite Gardaí and carrying military assault rifles were among a group that staged an audacious attack at the Regency Hotel in Whitehall, Dublin in broad daylight on February 5, 2016. They walked into a weigh-in for a boxing match, the WBO European Lightweight title, and starting shooting. David Byrne of the Kinehan cartel was shot dead and two others injured. The attack was part of an ongoing feud between the Kinehan and Hutch gangs that started with a shooting in Marbella, Spain in 2015 and has continued to the present day, costing 20 lives, including cases of mistaken identity.

To get a better understanding of the nature of crime in Ireland, I met with criminologist Professor Claire Hamilton of Maynooth University. I asked her about the roots of the gun culture which took off in the 1990s. She made the link with the spending craze that accompanied the Celtic Tiger. While people with money embraced a showy, materialistic lifestyle, many were left on the outside, looking in, with no legal route to achieving that ideal.

'The Celtic Tiger fostered this sense of anime and of normlessness, as if Irish society lost its way a little. With the wealth created by the boom came more inequality. Looking at organised crime in an Irish context, social deprivation is a big issue, especially in the context of the huge profits to be made from drugs. Crime provided an alternative way of achieving prestige and status for males in particular.'

The worst year overall for gangland killings in Ireland was 2006, near the peak of the economic boom, when 21 people were murdered.

The good guys?

But what about the other side of the coin, policing and the criminal justice system? The legislation introduced after the Guerin case gave the police significant new powers, which they have used extensively. New minimum mandatory sentences were introduced for drug offences. But because the most ruthless and powerful criminals are much harder to catch, small-time operators have borne the brunt of zero tolerance, according to Professor Hamilton.

The Garda Síochána has lost considerable credibility since

the 1990s. Scandals in recent years include manipulated data, persecuted whistle-blowers and discrepancies in the penalty points system for driving offences, to name but a few. The Central Statistics Office raised concerns about underreporting of crime by the Gardaí and now publishes those crime figures 'under reservation' to highlight their concerns about the quality of underlying data from the PULSE database.

Because many crimes are not reported by victims, the best measure of crime is victimisation surveys that ask people which, if any, crimes they have been the victim of in the previous 12 months. The most recent CSO survey from 2015 showed 8 per cent of households said they had been victims of household crime and 5 per cent said they had been victims of personal crime. Only 62 per cent of household crime and 54 per cent of all crimes against individuals had been reported to Gardaí, though other surveys put the reporting rate higher.

Let's look at the Garda figures. In 2018, there were 74 murders in Ireland, about 3,000 reported sexual offences, almost 20,000 attempts or threats to murder, assaults, harassment and related offences, 128 kidnapping and related offences and some 17,000 burglaries.

So how does this compare with crime rates in other countries? Recent comparative figures are hard to come by. In a 2012 report, Civitas, the British Institute for the Study of Civil Society, looked at different international data and came up with rankings of the incidence of various crimes. Bearing in mind what we know about reporting and recording, Ireland was high to mid-table out of 36 OECD countries.

Compared with the different parts of the UK, Ireland is not the worst:

Ranks out of 36 countries unless stated	England	Scotland	Northern Ireland	Ireland
Homicide	22nd	12th	18th	20th
Rape	5th out of 34	11th	8th	23rd
Robbery	7th	23rd	13th	18th
Assault (resulting in serious injury)	3rd	1st	28th	10th
Burglary	7th	22nd	12th	16th

Source: Civitas.org.uk [viii]

The threat of terrorism that overshadowed the Irish State during the Troubles had a huge impact on policing in Ireland, as well as on the Department of Justice. This became painfully clear in the damning Toland Report of 2014[ix]. The report's review group found the culture of the department to be closed and unnecessarily secretive and said that it had a deferential relationship towards the Garda Síochána. This tallies with the experience of Professor Hamilton:

'It is a product of the fact that the department was established in the context of subversive activity. Everything was connected to national security so it pervaded the entire culture when it came to ordinary crime. The same methods, defensiveness and secretiveness, applied. This has had interesting effects, bad and good in equal measure. The guards in many ways are the pivot around which the rest of the criminal justice system revolves.'

We have gone from a phase of boosting policing and investigative powers to a more critical examination of the work done by the Gardaí. There is a growing consensus that the force is in need of fundamental reform. The Commission on the Future of Policing, which reported in September 2018, has set out a new vision for the

Gardaí with a focus on community policing. Among many issues raised, the commission's chairperson, Kathleen O'Toole, said it was clear that 'the current arrangements for overseeing the police and investigating complaints are complex and confused'.[x]

Shortly before the report was released, the Irish Council for Civil Liberties launched its own report by the former human rights advisor to the Policing Board of Northern Ireland, Alyson Fitzpatrick, on how to implement a human-rights based approach to Garda reform.

Kilpatrick found there was a serious gap in human-rights compliance in a number of areas including the policing of protest, investigation of hate crime, stop-and-search practices, state security, and the treatment of people in Garda detention.[xi]

At least there are still ample reserves of goodwill towards the men and women in navy. Nine out of ten Irish people still have mid to high trust in the Gardaí, according to the Garda public attitudes survey[xii]. The same proportion felt they would be treated with respect in interactions with Gardaí. This current focus on weaknesses in management and systems can only be a good thing, sunlight being the best disinfectant.

The real fighting Irish

Irish athletes have brought home a modest haul of Olympic medals over the years, and it is remarkable that more than half of those medals, 16, were won by boxers. For that reason, and because of their equal success in the professional sport, lots of Irish boxers have become household names. People like Katie Taylor, Steve Collins, Michael Carruth, Wayne McCollough, Michael Conlon, Andy Lee and, of course, Barry McGuigan are widely admired.

These are the real fighting Irish and their success is part of a long tradition of Irish people and people of Irish descent being drawn to the sport, often in the absence of other opportunities. The Irish connections are as old as the sport. Irish-American John L. Sullivan was recognised as the first heavyweight champion of gloved boxing in 1892 and the last heavyweight champion of bare-knuckle boxing.

The Irish fighter who has grabbed the most column inches and prize money is Mixed Martial Arts champion and former boxer Conor McGregor. The Dubliner plays heavily on his national identity, adopting a clownish angry Irish persona to the delight of his fans. McGregor seems to crave notoriety, inside or outside the ring or cage, and has been prosecuted in the US for disorderly conduct. But McGregor's behaviour is not typical.

Olympic gold-medallist and current undisputed lightweight female world champion Katie Taylor is a better ambassador for her country. Universally liked, she is considered one of the most talented Irish sportspeople currently in competition. There is more to the Bray woman than the desire for victories and accolades. In an interview with the International Boxing Association, she gave her favourite quote as the following lines from Psalm 18.

'It is God who arms me with strength
and keeps my way secure.
He makes my feet like the feet of a deer;
He causes me to stand on the heights.
He trains my hands for battle;'

Endnotes

[i] Remarks by President Trump at the 2019 Presentation of the Shamrock Bowl, published on WhiteHouse.gov, 15.03.2019

[ii] From an article, 'Irish in America', published in Dickens's magazine, *All the Year Round*, 01.05.1869

[iii] *The American Irish: A Political and Social Portrait*, William V. Shannon, University of Massachusetts Press, p.17

[iv] Landy, M. (2000). *The International Cast of Irish Cinema: The Case of Michael Collins*, boundary 2, 27(2), 21-44. Duke University Press. Retrieved 23.03.2019, from Project MUSE database.

[v] Belfast Child website of victims, belfastchildis.com

[vi] 'These are the names of some of the 3,637 people whose lives and violent deaths are recorded in an extraordinary new book', *The Independent*, 12.10.1999

[vii] 'Last of John Gilligan's property sold by Criminal Assets Bureau', *The Irish Times*, 21.11.2018

[viii] Civitas Crime: Comparisons of Crime in OECD Countries, CIVITAS Institute for the Study of Civil Society, Author: Nick Cowen, 2010

[ix] Report of the Independent Review Group on the Department of Justice and Equality, 11.07.2014

[x] The Future of Policing in Ireland report, by the Commission on the Future of Policing in Ireland, 18.09.2018

[xi] Human Rights Based Policing in Ireland, by the Irish Council for Civil Liberties, 14.09.2018

[xii] An Garda Síochána Public Attitudes Survey Bulletin, Q4 2018, research conducted by amárach research

CHAPTER 3

The Irish have a Drink Problem

'When things go wrong and will not come right,
Though you do the best you can,
When life looks black as the hour of night,
A pint of plain is your only man.'

Flann O'Brien (Brian O'Nolan), from 'The Workman's
Friend' poem in *At Swim Two Birds* (1939)

'For those Irishmen whose hard drinking has made this
national trait proverbial in America, there has been an
also large, but little-noticed, number of men who were
teetotallers and of women whose detestation of the liquor
habit among their menfolk was strong and abiding.[i]'

William V. Shannon, historian 1989

'Ireland sober is Ireland free.'

19th century temperance movement slogan

'Are you taking the Pledge?' That was what everyone wanted
to know ahead of my Confirmation ceremony, a big deal which
marks the end of primary school for Irish Catholics. A remnant
of the temperance movements that began in the 19th century, the
pledge to abstain from alcohol until a certain age – 18 or 21 – was
taken silently at a given moment in the ceremony. We children
were asked to look into our hearts and pledge to avoid the demon

drink, which most of us obligingly did. At 11 years of age, alcohol held no special interest for me and I made the promise freely. The Pledge has survived in some form for the current generation, though it is generally offered at a pre-Confirmation ceremony and now includes a promise to avoid drugs too.

The fact that alcohol is a topic for children of this age in Irish society is an expression of a deep-rooted anxiety about drink, which goes back a long way. The most famous Irish crusader against alcohol was Father Theobold Matthew whose temperance campaign went viral in the middle of the 19th century. By some estimates he succeeded in enrolling more than half the adult population in his mass movement.

Ordained in 1814, Father Matthew worked among the poor in Cork city and became increasingly dismayed at the suffering caused by alcohol abuse. While the Catholic Church was inclined to recommend moderation rather than abstinence, Father Matthew was convinced that more drastic action was required. He founded the Cork Total Abstinence Society in 1838 and was the first to take the pledge to abstain from alcohol for life. The Tipperary-born priest became a national sensation, with tens of thousands of people turning up to his temperance rallies to sign the pledge. The crime rate dropped dramatically in a short space of time, along with whiskey consumption. However, lacking a proper organisational structure at a national level, the movement fell apart in the wider social collapse of the Famine.

The culture of excessive drinking never went away and Father James Cullen took up the baton in 1898, founding the Pioneer Total Abstinence Association. Catholics flocked to join and the organisation reached its peak in the 1950s, by which time one in three Irish adults were members. Today, there are

100,000 Pioneers in Ireland, identifiable by the Pioneer pin they wear as part of their pledge. Catholic organisations aside, the enduring abstinence ethos is an important part of the picture in understanding Irish drinking. One in five Irish people currently lives alcohol free. Some estimates say as many as one in four.

By 14, I had outgrown the Pledge as inevitably as my confirmation outfit. All around was a thriving drinking culture into which I felt an urgent need to be initiated. Ireland was in the middle of an alcohol consumption boom, especially among the young, with intake increasing threefold between 1960 and 2001 when it reached a peak of 14.3 litres of alcohol per year per person aged 15 or over. My first night consuming alcohol was my first night drunk. Following my older sister's instructions, I filled a small lemonade bottle with neat spirits, drams stolen from several bottles so as not to be noticed. The mix was known to us as snakebite and I drank it with friends at one of the many outdoor drinking spots, Mullin's Hill.

By 15, I could get served in some bars in the locality known for turning a blind eye to underage drinkers. All I had to do was memorise a legal date of birth and hide behind my backcombed fringe. By this stage my tipple was gin and blackcurrant, an idea copied from an older, more sophisticated neighbour. When we went to school discos, we drank a few bottles of Ritz or Stag behind a gatepost nearby before we queued up. The braver ones smuggled in a naggin of vodka. We were all in training to be binge drinkers and some would go further than others along this road.

As well as Ireland being ranked seventh globally in terms of overall alcohol consumption, binge drinking is a particular problem in Ireland. According to the World Health Organisation's 2018 global status report on alcohol and health, 38 per cent of Irish people aged 15 and over had engaged in heavy episodic drinking in the past 30 days [ii]. This placed Irish drinkers in eleventh position globally.

'Out Out'

One striking statistic from an Irish Health Research Board survey shows that one in eight (13%) men and almost one in ten (9%) women drank the full amount of their recommended weekly guidelines in one sitting in the week prior to the survey. Among 18- to 24-year-old men and women, the rate was 28 per cent and 22 per cent respectively.

These are people like the characters in *Oh My God What a Complete Aisling*, the bestselling 2018 novel by Emer McLysaght and Sarah Breen. There are numerous binge drinking scenes in the book which is set in contemporary Ireland, featuring characters in their twenties. In one scene about halfway through the story, our heroine Aisling is encouraged to join her friend Majella on a mid-week night out. They meet first at Majella's house.

'Majella got two bottles of wine in Centra. Dear ones. €11 each. "We're worth it," she said as she pulled them out of her handbag. She's poured us a pint of wine each to have with our chicken Kievs (feck the points).'

Majella is a secondary school teacher who is drinking to a dangerous extent without anyone around her batting an eyelid. Excessive drinking is indulged as an amusing personality trait in the book, much as in real life among this age group. Aisling explains that Majella makes a distinction between going Out and going Out Out.

'Out is a couple of pints of Coors Light in The Big Tree or The Foggy Dew, last bus home, maybe a bag of chips if the hunger is at you. Out Out is roaring along to "Jump Around" at 1 a.m. spilling vodka and Diet Coke down your work shirt.'

On the night of the chicken Kievs, the girls end up drinking a pint-and-a-half of wine at home, go out to a bar where they switch to vodka and Diet Coke and round off the night with several Baby Guinness shots (coffee liqueur with a head of Irish cream).

In real life, binge drinking by young women like Aisling and Majella takes place all over Ireland. Excessive drinking is also an integral part of watching and playing sport. The Gaelic Athletic Association (GAA) tried to curtail drinking among players by introducing long pre-match drinking bans. But this has had the effect of encouraging wild bouts of drinking between bans. Galway hurler Joe Canning responded to the controversial policy in an interview with balls.ie.[iii]

'The culture in the GAA is for lads to go on the piss for a day or two after a big game. And that's totally wrong for your body and for your mind. They end up sick for nearly a week afterwards because they feel they have to go ballistic. I'm not for a second recommending a drink culture, but the balance is so wrong.'

Based on the latest research, 'more than 150,000 Irish people are dependent drinkers, more than 1.35 million are harmful drinkers, and 30 per cent of people interviewed say that they experienced some form of harm as a result of their own drinking'.[iv]

These sobering statistics raise the question why. Why this tendency to drink to excess more than other nationalities? In the past it could arguably be blamed on a need to escape from the misery of poverty and oppression. Yet consumption of alcohol reached its highest levels this century during recent periods of prosperity. Something very powerful is going on in terms of self-image, as sociologist Geraldine Moane writes in her essay 'Post-colonial legacies and the Irish psyche' for the collection *Are the Irish Different?*

'The view of the Irish as heavy drinkers, as alcoholic, as dysfunctional with regard to alcohol, is one of the most recurring in popular culture and in the literature.'[v]

The idea of drinking being part of who we are is continually reinforced and has been internalised by Irish people. The advertising repertoire of well-known Irish alcohol brands has made no small contribution to this mindset, as has the proliferation of Irish pubs worldwide. When US presidents come to Ireland, they are dragged along to a pub to be photographed with a pint of Guinness. In British television drama, Irish actors tend to get bit parts as the local drunkard. Certainly, it is the most frequent stereotype I am confronted with as an Irish person abroad. I have lost count of the number of times in social situations where people I've just met refer to my readiness to drink or my capacity to drink, before I've even taken a sip. Friends do it too. And when I am the first to drain my glass and look for more, which tends to happen more often in Switzerland, I feel helpless to contradict the stereotype. The same weight of expectation exists in Ireland, especially among young people who are under pressure not just to have fun but to be fun through alcohol. 'Thus "the Irish as drinkers" operates as a perception by others, as an identity or internalised self-perception, and as behavioural and cultural patterns, creating a self-perpetuating cycle,' Moane concludes.

If the cap fits

Unsurprisingly there is no shortage of famous role models for the stereotypical Irish drunk, a volatile rogue, though it must be said they are all male and mostly deceased. Brendan Behan, who playfully described himself as a drinker with writing problems, became a legend in his own time but paid the ultimate price by dying at the age of 41. The actor Richard Harris was known for running out onto the road when he was drinking and throwing punches at cars. Shane MacGowan of The Pogues is suffering the effects of years of uncontrolled drinking during which he became more famous for public drunkenness than for his music.

These iconic figures are the tip of the cultural iceberg, with endless representations of drunken Irish characters in film, music and literature at home and abroad. Even popular American cartoon series poke fun at Irish clichés, repeatedly in the case of *The Simpsons*. In one St. Patrick's Day episode, the newsreader Kent Brockman (Kent O'Brockman for the occasion) is making a live broadcast at the town parade when he is surrounded by a group of brawling revellers. For the sake of the joke, Brockman reacts as if their behaviour is a travesty and appeals to them to stop. Then, addressing the viewers, he says:

'Ladies and gentlemen, what you're seeing is a total disregard for what St Patrick's Day stands for. All this drinking, violence, destruction of property, are these the things we think of when we think of the Irish?'

When *Family Guy* set an episode in Ireland[vi], the arrival scene shows the talking dog and his master in the plane as the captain announces 'welcome to Ireland'. The two passengers have the following exchange:

Peter Griffin: 'This is quite a country, Brian. You know Ireland has more drunks per capita than people.'

Brian the dog: 'Oh that's a negative stereotype. I don't think the Irish drink as much as people say they do.'

Cue the next shot of the plane landing on the runway which is carpeted knee-deep in empty beer bottles. I have to laugh at both jokes but, dear God, it's getting a bit old. Irish-themed Hollywood films routinely feature heavy drinking or violence, or both, all the way back to *The Quiet Man* and beyond.

Back in the real world, Frank McCourt's alcoholic father in his memoir *Angela's Ashes* represents the worst manifestation of the Irish drunk, the abusive and neglectful parent. Malachy McCourt drank his wages or dole money, leading his family to utter destitution. Alcohol is still a significant contributory factor for child neglect today, according to Alcohol Action Ireland. A national audit of neglect cases found that 62 per cent of cases resulted from alcohol abuse.

While drinking in a group may be fun in the middle part of the night, drunkenness can turn nasty at the end of a night out. There is the nuisance factor of noise and people urinating in public but also more serious concerns such as the risk of drink driving or violence. With a high number of drunk people congregating near pubs, clubs and fast-food outlets at closing time, everyone's safety is at risk. The worst is when people do not feel safe in their own home because of the volatile behaviour of an intoxicated family member. Alcohol is also a factor in half of all suicides in Ireland.

Alcohol Action Ireland, an independent national charity for alcohol-related issues, put together a grim round-up of the harmful effects of alcohol. It is a long list, beginning with the fact that alcohol is a factor in the vast majority of public order offences and in many assaults, including sexual assaults, rape and domestic violence and manslaughter. And then there is the effect on health. Every day, 1,500 hospital beds are occupied by people with alcohol-related problems. 'The total cost of alcohol-related discharges from hospital was €1.5 billion in 2012, which is equal to €1 for every €10 spent on public health.' And that's not counting the significant costs of emergency cases, GP visits, psychiatric admissions and alcohol treatment services.

Obviously policymakers cannot sit by and do nothing in the face of this problem. Pricing has been used before to reduce demand with some success. Perhaps the greatest untold story about Irish drinking is that consumption per capita has fallen substantially since the peak of 2001, from 14.3 litres of pure alcohol to 11.46 litres in 2016 (though it is creeping up again). Ireland has one of the highest alcohol excise duties in Europe, much to the chagrin of the drinks industry, which reluctantly collects €2.3 billion per year in excise and VAT revenue for the Exchequer.[vii]

Ireland has the highest wine excise duty in the EU (80 cent per 187 ml), the second highest beer excise, and the third highest spirits excise, ranking alongside Finland, Sweden and the UK. Alcohol is also subject to VAT at 23 per cent. The Drinks Industry Group of Ireland is calling for the excise duty to be lowered but they haven't an ice cube's chance in a hot whiskey of seeing this happen.

The Public Health (Alcohol) Bill is the latest attempt to tackle alcohol abuse through legislation. Passed in October 2018, the bill took three years to crawl through the Oireachtas (parliament); a small group of rural TDs tried to filibuster up to the last minute. But Health Minister Simon Harris was finally able to enact the legislation with the main elements intact. He gave a frank assessment of the problem.

'We are legislating for alcohol as it affects our health... we know we have a relationship with alcohol in this country that is not good, that damages our health, that harms our community. This will help to change the culture of drinking in Ireland over a period of time.'

Designed to make alcohol less attractive, the measures include a minimum price per unit of alcohol, restrictions on advertising, and stark health warning labels, similar to the scary warnings on cigarette packets. These deterrents will be implemented in stages but will they have any effect on the lifestyle of people drawn to heavy drinking? We won't know for several years.

The Irish pub

We are all agreed that drinking has its dark side but it has been a core part of community celebration, daily life and trade since ancient times. Irish mythology features many banquets where cups were passed round the company. Along with domestically-produced mead and ale, our distant ancestors drank wine which was imported from the Continent as far back as pre-Christian times. Medieval monks introduced distilling to Ireland and whiskey was first produced commercially beginning in the 17th century. A recent detailed study of the early modern Irish diet by historian Susan Flavin revealed that, alongside bread, beer was the most important dietary staple of the 16th century.

Records from Dublin Castle showed that the household staff consumed 264,000 pints of beer in 1590, which averaged up to eight pints each per day. 'Domestic brewing was seen as the role of the housewife, and there are also records of women and children joining labourers to drink together at the end of the working day. At Dublin Castle there are even records of "drinkings" which took place in the main entertaining area of the castle and were ladies-only events.'[viii]

Irish pubs now fulfil the purpose of giving people a place to gather and drink, and we are spoilt for choice with so many convivial places vying for our custom. When I was 16, I got a part-time job as a lounge girl in one of the busiest pubs in my area. Kitted out in a black skirt and white shirt, I walked to work three evenings a week to join a team of up to six girls. We lined the tin tray with beermats to soak up the spills, grabbed a glass for the float and set off to do the circuit of the pub all evening.

Despite the noise and the smoke, I liked the pub. To me, it was a cheerful place full of people enjoying each other's company. It seemed to be the essence of adulthood. Most Irish drinking was taking place in this setting, not at home. I couldn't wait to become a legal customer myself.

By the time I was legally old enough to drink (18), I was attending college in Dublin city centre and had about half a dozen favourite watering holes. Frequenting those old pubs was a way of connecting with a notion of a romantic past I had in my head, a literary, masculine past that drew me in and seemed to offer me a place too. Along the way, I trained myself to like Guinness, part of this essential Irish identity I wanted to express. In my part-time job I had progressed to working behind the bar, and between my work shifts and socialising, I spent most evenings in some pub or other. It became my natural habitat. Because I was on a low budget, my drinking was not excessive. A more harmful phase of drinking would come later in my twenties, when more disposable income meant more hangovers and occasional alcohol-related blackouts.

I suspect the classic partying lifestyle of the twenty-something is often tinged with desperation, not just in my case. It is one way to cope with separation from the family unit and a lack of security in work, relationships and housing. When your life seems to be full of sharp edges, drink smoothes them down, for a few hours at least.

I wasn't the only one who enjoyed spending time in Irish pubs but it has always been a challenge for pubs to compete with each other. There are some 7,200 licensed bars operating in Ireland today, half the number that existed a century ago but still a much greater density of pubs than anywhere in the UK, for example. The smaller and more casual businesses have fallen by the wayside and there is pressure on publicans despite good potential for profit. Tony Morrissey of Morrissey's auctioneering and consultancy firm gave an insight into the sector in his contribution to an AIB report on the licenced trade in 2018.[ix]

'If a pub is not turning over €8,000-€9,000 a week in rural areas, then it's going to be very difficult for them to survive. The same is true of Dublin and if a pub [there] is not turning over between €12,000-€13,000 a week, it's in trouble.'

Flat-packed craic

Who would have thought 30 years ago that the formula for an Irish pub could be decoded and turned into a successful export? Remarkably, there are now more Irish pubs outside Ireland than at home. The global spread of Irish pubs is largely a post-1990 phenomenon which has given us a force of at least 8,500 Irish pubs, like alternative embassies, in every corner of the world (152 countries and counting).

One key part of the formula is the concept of 'craic', a widely used Irish word for fun and merriment. Strictly speaking, craic is not something that can be manufactured or distributed but the same can be said of any of the intangible things people are sold, from prestige to purity. Investors in Irish pubs abroad pay to recreate the setting in which craic is supposedly experienced in Ireland. The combination of bric-a-brac, dark wood, drinking songs and vintage posters is meant to work its magic on customers. Even if the magic doesn't happen, an Irish pub, whether it's in Singapore or Siberia, promises a pleasant and familiar refuge which has its own attraction.

Mulligans pub in Dublin city centre. This pub is mentioned by James Joyce in *The Dubliners*.

There had always been Irish-dominated pubs in cities with a big Irish population. But that meant only in traditional destination countries for Irish emigrants. In Britain, pubs were considered Irish by virtue of the fact that they were frequented by an Irish crowd. They didn't necessarily have a bespoke Irish interior. Similarly, in the United States, Irish pubs were mostly neighbourhood bars frequented by Irish immigrants, although there were some venerable old establishments founded by Irish immigrants that cultivated an Irish-style décor. Places like McSorley's Old Ale House in East Village, New York, established in 1854, or J.J. Foley's in Boston, set up by Kerryman Jeremiah Foley in 1909.

So how did the Irish pub become the country's largest cultural export? How did we move from Irish emigrants pursuing their own business plans in an organic way to the proliferation of custom-made Irish pubs we have today? The answer lies in the power of Ireland's iconic black drink. Guinness Brewing Company was indeed the driving force, best placed to spot the trend and scale it up. In the late 1980s and early 1990s they noticed a spike in sales each time an Irish pub opened abroad, firstly with the almost guaranteed success of the pub itself, and secondly through other bars in the area offering Guinness as a response to that success.

'It seemed that no matter where somebody placed an Irish Pub, it became instantly successful. Out of this observation grew a question... if someone could define the critical factors that made these pubs so successful, could investors be found to apply the critical factors and so open many more pubs globally?'[x]

Guinness set up the Irish Pub Concept, teaming up with players who were already providing a pub creation service on a modest scale. Mel McNally, one of Guinness' first partners, was at the forefront of the marketing phenomenon when he set up The Irish Pub Company in 1990. McNally's interest in the sector was sparked by a research project on old Irish pubs he worked on as an architecture student in the 1970s. By the 1980s he was creating classical designs for pubs in Ireland and the UK, inspired by the 'Great Old Irish Pubs' he had studied. With Guinness, McNally developed six pub styles for the catalogue: Shop, Gastro, Victorian, Brewery, Country and Celtic. Aspiring publicans around the world were guided through the process of setting up an Irish pub, and provided with all the materials, made in Ireland. These days The Irish Pub Company is one of four similar companies working with Guinness' Irish Pub Concept.

One of those companies, ÓL Irish Pubs, boasts a warehouse full of authentic Irish bric-a-brac and memorabilia that they are constantly adding to. Once the design is agreed on, they make all the furniture and fixtures in their Irish joinery workshop – Victorian, Brewery, Country or Chemist. From the signing of the contract, ÓL can deliver a completed bar build within 16 weeks.

They ship everything in containers and send out fitters, joiners, painters and tilers to turn the prepared shell into an authentic Irish pub. Rumours of the demise of the Irish pub have yet to be proved true. The formula is still going strong, with the pub companies now providing makeovers ('health checks') for ageing pubs.

A pint of plain

Guinness is Ireland's strongest brand of all time, ranked the country's most valuable brand by the consultancy Brand Finance in 2019, worth €2.5 billion. In its advertising campaigns it taps into a storied representation of Irishness as something pure, authentic and mystical. The 2018 'Bound Together' campaign as part of their sponsorship of the GAA championship is a perfect example, mixing drone shots of the Irish landscape with behind the scenes sporting atmosphere. The voiceover talks about the unifying force of the 'people, family, communities' and goes on to say that 'this [the GAA] is more than an association; we are bound together'. The final shot is the Guinness Harp against a black background with the caption 'Made of More'.

Just as the GAA is more than an association, Guinness is more than a drink, ever since Arthur Guinness signed a 9,000-year lease for the St James's Gate Brewery in 1759. The business quickly became a success, specialising in porter, and was passed on from father to son for a remarkable five generations. By the 1830s it became the largest brewery in Ireland, by the turn of the 20th century, the largest in the world. In 1997 Guinness Plc merged with Grand Metropolitan Plc in a £24 billion deal, forming a new company called Diageo Plc.

You can learn all this if you go to the Guinness Storehouse in Dublin, Ireland's most popular tourist attraction. Ascending the seven floors of the museum is a Brave New World-like experience, with warm, insistent voices constantly extolling the wonders of Guinness.

The Storehouse is the jewel in the crown of Ireland's alcohol-tourism sector. Plenty of other brands, especially whiskeys, are harnessing an Irish *je ne sais quoi* to sell drinks. Irish whiskey is one of the fastest growing attractions in Irish tourism, with eight new distillery visitor centres due to open in 2019, to add to the 13 already in existence. The distilleries recorded almost a million visitors in 2018 and are aiming to increase visitor numbers to 1.9 million in 2025, as set out in the Irish Whiskey Tourism Strategy.

As I've worked on this chapter, it has been disconcerting to recognise the influence of a commodified version of Irishness on my own relationship with alcohol over the years. I am left with a niggling sense of having been groomed by an unseen master of ceremonies. When I worked in Irish pubs in Paris in the 1990s, I myself was part of the marketing model. One of the seven critical success factors identified by the Irish Pub Concept was the importance of key Irish staff 'to help promote an authentic pub culture'. I played the part perfectly: I was friendly, I was welcoming, I was happy to stay late after work and drink. The popular walking pub tours of Dublin are a close copy of my own personal map of favourite pubs from my youth. How much does my student-era quest for belonging in the vintage pubs of Dublin differ from what tourists are looking for today? When I took the Pledge as a child, little did I know that I would soon be handed a licence to drink, and that this invitation was part of a stronger tradition based on my nationality. That any drinking I partook in would be encouraged and endorsed by the wider culture in literature, film, advertising and song. And that I would see casualties to that tradition along the way.

Endnotes

---

[i] *The American Irish: A Political and Social Portrait*, William V. Shannon, University of Massachusetts Press, p. 21

[ii] Heavy episodic drinking is defined as having consumed 60 grams or more of pure alcohol on at least one occasion in the past 30 days (WHO definition)

[iii] 'Eddie Brennan speaks absolute sense about drinking bans in the GAA', by Gavin Cooney, balls.ie, 10.01.2018

[iv] alcoholireland.ie/facts/how-much-do-we-drink/

[v] *Are the Irish Different?* edited by Tom Inglis, Manchester University Press, 2014, Chapter: Post-colonial legacies and the Irish psyche by Geraldine Moane, p. 127

[vi] 'Peter's two Dads', Season five, Episode ten, 11.02.2007

[vii] http://www.drinksindustry.ie/news/news-and-press/ireland-ranks-second-in-eu-big-4-for-highest-alcohol-excise-tax-new-report/ 05.09.2018

[viii] https://aru.ac.uk/news/the-important-role-of-beer-in-16th-century-ireland 11.10.2017

[ix] https://business.aib.ie/help/outlook-pubs-2018, February 2018

[x] http://irishpubconcept.com/about/overview/

CHAPTER 4

The Irish are Great Writers

Is acher ingáith innocht fufuasna faireggae findfolt ni ágor réimm
mora minn dondláechraid lainn ua lothlind

'Bitter is the wind tonight, it tosses the ocean's white hair
I fear not the coursing of a clear sea by the fierce warriors
from Lothlend'[i]

These words in Old Irish run along the top of a page of a Latin grammar manuscript dating from the ninth century, the Priscian manuscript of St. Gallen. *Lothlind*, land of the lakes, is an early form of the Irish word for Scandinavia, more specifically Norway. The fierce warriors kept at bay by the weather are Viking raiders.

The unknown scribe who wrote these lines lived in dangerous times. We don't know exactly what scriptorium he worked in, but two possible locations are the monasteries of Bangor or Nendrum in County Down, both of which suffered heavily under Viking attacks in the ninth and tenth centuries. The monks would have breathed easier on stormy days.

I love the idea of the obedient monk faithfully transcribing page after page of intricate text for months or years, working for the community, for learning, for God. And then, one dreary day, he feels the urge to write something heartfelt and original. He throws caution to the wind and allows himself a brief moment of creative expression. That brief moment of inspiration survives more than a millennium.

Irish writers are still answering the call, in ever increasing numbers. The first laureate of Irish fiction, Anne Enright, has described the Irish desire to write as a cultural disease. Speaking to Miriam O'Callaghan on RTÉ Radio[ii], she joked that there were at least three people in Ireland who didn't want to write a novel.

So why do so many of us get infected? A lot of it comes from growing up in a culture where writers are revered. We have embraced the idea that this is what Irish success looks like. In the first rocky decades of independence, when the country often felt like a failed experiment, the global success of artists such as George Bernard Shaw, James Joyce, William Butler Yeats and Samuel Beckett provided proof that we were clever. We basked in the reflected glory, ignoring the fact that the State was using draconian censorship powers to oppress a new generation of writers. But the tendency to lionise writers endured while the fanatical fear of 'indecency' gradually subsided. Eventually, even those who had spent their best years banned got the recognition and respect they deserved.

Our four Nobel prize-winners for literature – Yeats, Shaw, Beckett and Seamus Heaney – are still a bulwark against any lingering postcolonial doubts about Irish aptitude. And we still celebrate our beloved literary ancestors. We name planes, ferries, pubs and housing estates after them. Until recently, we concentrated on a select cast of heroes at the expense of the wider community. Think of them as the twelve apostles of Irish writing – the four giants already named, along with Jonathan Swift, Oliver Goldsmith, Oscar Wilde, John Millington Synge, Sean O'Casey, Patrick Kavanagh, Flann O'Brien and Brendan Behan (the latter two also wrote in Irish). The twelve are famously grouped together in the black-and-white poster of Irish writers that is a staple in the décor of Ireland's other major cultural export – the Irish pub.

What was originally a quiet pride in their greatness has become pretty noisy. These dead Irish writers did not escape the commodification of Irish culture that took off in the 1990s, far from it. They are a core part of the national brand, being flogged in every imaginable scrap of merchandise from fridge magnets to coasters. Their names are worn out from overuse in self-congratulatory marketing copy in a way that not one of them would have appreciated, I imagine. All in the service of convincing ourselves and others that the Irish are great writers.

But that does not mean that Ireland has always been a great place for writers. The cold hand of the censor cut the best Irish writers off from their readers in a cruel and debilitating way from the 1930s to the end of the 1960s. When Edna O'Brien was asked in a BBC interview in 1965 if she would find it possible to live and write in Ireland, she had a pretty cutting response: 'I'd find it possible to live if I suppressed at least nine tenths of my nature. If I wanted to live there like a cow or a stone, I suppose I could live there very happily.'[iii]

O'Brien is one of a long line of writers who found Ireland too stifling to live in, for practical or artistic reasons. Some – like Shaw, Yeats, Synge and Oscar Wilde – went away (for shorter or longer periods) because their Anglo-Irish background made Britain and select parts of the Continent a natural extension of their cultural space. Others, like Joyce and O'Brien, were driven by an urge for freedom and the need to make a living. There is no mistaking the passion in James Joyce's words, spoken by Stephen Dedalus to his friend Cranly in *A Portrait of the Artist as a Young Man*:

'I will tell you what I will do and what I will not do. I will not serve that in which I no longer believe, whether it calls itself my home, my fatherland, or my church: and I will try to express myself in some mode of life or art as freely as I can and as wholly as I can, using for my defence the only arms I allow myself to use — silence, exile, and cunning.'[iv]

Sculpture of James Joyce by Milton Hebald at his grave in Fluntern cemetary, Zurich. His wife Nora Barnacle wished to have his remains repatriated but such was the hostility to Joyce among the Irish political and religious establishment that her request was refused.

Special case

At an April 2019 event honouring Belfast-born Booker prize-winner Anna Burns in the city's Lyric Theatre, Anne Enright said of Burns' book, *Milkman* (see **Chapter 6: The Irish want a United Ireland**): 'It has this amazing international reach. It manages that alchemy that Irish books are so good at, the turning of our difficulties and our shames into some strange kind of glory.'ᵛ

Is that the secret to Irish literary success – a unique brand of suffering that converts into great art with universal appeal? Where does that leave writers who came of age this century for whom Irish suffering, like the Irish lifestyle, has become less acute and more generic? To answer these questions, it is worth delving into the mystique that surrounds Irish writing talent.

If an Irish author is interviewed abroad, there is a good chance he or she will be asked or will volunteer something about the unique Irish culture of storytelling. The great oral tradition might be mentioned. But doesn't almost every culture have a significant oral tradition which came before literacy when that was the only way to hand down the tales that helped people understand where they came from?

What is so special about the case of Ireland? There are some things, though it is debatable how many of them are relevant to a writer born in the second half of the 20ᵗʰ century. For argument's sake, you could identify five main factors that have influenced the Irish literary tradition: the survival of an ancient, indigenous mythology; the special place of the poet or bard in Gaelic society; the lost language; the colonial pressure on behaviour and communication; and finally, the influence of the Catholic Church on Irish literature which deserves its own chapter.

Let's go back to the monk who wrote the Viking poem. When the Latin alphabet was used to write the native language, it opened up a new vista for secular learning. The monks didn't just produce grammars, gospels and other holy books. They also recorded the heroic sagas of pre-Christian Ireland, which are partly historically based. These give us a rich picture of Celtic society and customs, which all but disappeared from mainland Europe in the Dark

Ages. So it is that the oldest vernacular literature (written in the native language rather than Latin) in western Europe is in Irish.

At the time of the Priscian manuscript there was an aristocratic class of professional poets, *filid*, whose job it was to know and preserve the tales and genealogies of the ruling classes, as well as to compose their own poems. To reach the highest grade of seven grades, the *filid* had to study for 12 years and memorise hundreds of stories and poems. For this great achievement they had the honour of trimming their cloaks with bird feathers. The social importance of these poets declined and ultimately vanished along with the old Gaelic social order in the 17th century.

But the tradition of storytelling survived in a more informal way through the *seanchaí*, wandering storytellers who peddled their stories from place to place. And communities continued to value their oral storytellers even when literacy spread. Even now, a person known for their storytelling skills might be referred to in a complimentary way as a *seanchaí*. There is a small grassroots movement trying to revive the tradition by holding gatherings for storytelling. The Sneem Storytelling Festival in County Kerry, for example, has been on the go since 2012.

What about the lost or almost lost language? Irish is the first official language of Ireland (English second) and is taught as a compulsory subject in all primary and secondary schools. However, according to the last census, only 73,803 people spoke the language daily outside the education system. Irish is not closely related to English, which is a Germanic language overlaid with Romance influences from the conquering Normans. As one of the Celtic group of languages, Irish is no closer to English than the Slavic languages or any other group of Indo-European languages. This is important to point out because of the common misconception abroad that the Irish language is a dialect of

English. It is also relevant that, coming from a different group, the Irish language configures the world quite differently to English.

Many respected writers continued to create literature in Irish – poets like Nuala Ní Dhómhnaill and Máirtín Ó Direáin, and writers like Máirtín Ó Cadhain and Pádraig Ó Conaire. However, only a small number of people are proficient enough in Irish to read these writers' works in the original language. The vast majority of Irish writers today write in English and that will not change. But the bones of Irish can still be seen under the skin of the English spoken in Ireland – in syntax, cadence, vocabulary and of course accent. Although English is not a foreign language any more, the blending and colouring seen in the Irish brand of English can add originality to an Irish writer's use of the language.

The colonial influence is another special feature that has faded with time in the Republic and will continue to fade. In his collection of essays, *The Irish Story*, R.F. Foster talks about 'the necessary stratagems of irony, collusion and misdirection which accompany a colonized culture' as some of the factors that give 'a distinctive twist to the way the Irish account for themselves'[vi]. What is sometimes called blarney.

As for the Catholic Church in Ireland, the repressive sexual morality it imposed on the older generation can hardly be understood by those who did not live through it. This had an unavoidable effect on the inner life of young thinkers, either turning them into rebels or tortured souls.

A man I once interviewed who was born in the 1930s movingly described the struggle he experienced with scrupulosity, pathological guilt about religious issues, in his youth. 'The Church for me was a thing of fear, always. Because the preachers went on and on about hell and damnation and it overshadowed everything. We used to get regular sermons and retreats in school and every damn thing was about sexuality. At the age of 13 I didn't know the facts of life, I literally didn't. But I knew about mortal sin and for every impure thought I had, I went through a constant loop of worry, weighing up whether it fit the three-part definition of mortal sin.'

The all-pervasive influence of the Church was copper-fastened by its partnership with the State. Not only did the Church provide essential public services, it had an unofficial say in law-making. All this with the approval of civil society. These conditions of oppressive control gave writers an endless source of tragedy and conflict, sometimes mitigated by humour, fertile ground for fiction. The personal tragedies engendered by this culture revolve around familiar themes of abuse, disempowerment and injustice that are still prominent in contemporary writing today.

All this doom and gloom brings to mind one of the most enjoyable quotes from Yeats: 'Being Irish, he had an abiding sense of tragedy, which sustained him through temporary periods of joy'.

In my own experience, something I specifically miss living abroad is the Irish way of conversation which is much more story based than anything I've encountered in Switzerland, Russia, France or the United States. I yearn for the kind of company where people will naturally assume the role of entertaining each other by passing stories back and forth. I have learned that my efforts to dig for stories from Swiss people produce bafflement on both sides and scant results.

The Swiss correspondent of the national broadcaster, Martin Allioth, who retired in 2019 after 35 years of reporting from Ireland, observed that the most notable thing about Irish people was their curiosity, which he described as innocent and almost childlike. Speaking in Bern in 2018, he said 'they have a completely different social life and a much greater circle of friends and acquaintances because with each person they meet, they ask questions, looking for information with which they can establish a connection'.[vii]

I guess that is a nice way of saying the Irish are nosy. That curiosity is the hallmark of a writer too, not something you need to suppress growing up in Irish society. Or, as the great advocate of eavesdropping, Maeve Binchy, put it: 'We don't like pauses and silences, we prefer talk and information and conversations that go on and on. So that means we are halfway there [to being a writer].'[viii]

The business of writing

Irish authors are almost as good as Irish horses when it comes to winning prizes in the UK. When Anna Burns won the Booker Prize for Fiction in 2018, Sally Rooney and Donal Ryan were on the longlist. That made 3 Irish writers out of 13 in a prize open to writers of any nationality, writing in English and published in the UK and Ireland. (It must be said that Burns ticks both boxes of Irish and British.)

Sally Rooney became the youngest ever winner of the Costa Novel Award in 2018 for her second novel, *Normal People*, a moving account of a disjointed relationship between two lonely, young souls who keep too much hidden from each other. Rooney was following in the footsteps of fellow countryman Sebastian Barry who won the prize for the second time in 2017 for *Days Without End*, his seventh novel.

Other recent Irish award-winners include Sarah Crossan, Eimear McBride, Lisa McInerney, Danielle McLoughlin, Marina Carr, John Boyne and Mike McCormack. McCormack scooped the €100,000 International Dublin Literary Award in 2018 for *Solar Bones*. This is the peak of the writing business. But most authors will never receive a life-changing monetary award or the sales boost that comes with it. It has been speculated that only a dozen writers in Ireland can actually live from their books. Even John Banville, another Booker winner and national treasure, decided to adopt a nom de plume, Benjamin Black, and write a series of crime novels for commercial reasons.

Literary greatness is generally measured in sales, prizes and critical acclaim – though an author can be great but unrecognised for a multitude of reasons. But even when all those conditions are satisfied, as happened with Donal Ryan's debut in 2012, *The Spinning Heart*, the ultimate dream of making a living by writing alone usually remains just that, a dream. As Brendan Behan put it: 'The number of people who buy books in Ireland would not keep me in drink for the duration of the Sunday opening time'.

In truth, making a living by book sales is extremely rare, even when your home country has a large population. Most moderately successful Irish authors are obliged to fall back on related work, often in the various sub-sections of the writing economy such as editing, teaching, journalism, corporate writing or translation. Some, including Donal Ryan and Anne Enright, find a home in academia. Over time, writers may receive direct support to practise their craft, such as grants and residencies.

The insecurity of the writing life is nothing new and is not particular to Ireland. What is new is the speed of the market and the volume of titles constantly coming through. Authors with a new book have a horribly brief moment to shine before their precious work is swept away on the crowded conveyor belt, possibly never to be seen again.

A favourable habitat

The consolation is that there is a strong community spirit among writers in Ireland. Since the days when Edna O'Brien began her career, the habitat of Irish writers has become infinitely more bountiful. Censorship, which blighted so many careers and broke the natural link between Irish writers and their rightful readers, is a distant memory. Writers are celebrated in their lifetimes, which makes a nice change. What used to be called indecency is no longer feared but expected and appreciated by readers.

The challenge the Irish writer of today must face is to avoid distraction in a country that has become a literary wonderland. There were close to 70 literary festivals happening in 2019, including heavies like Listowel Writers' Week and the Bloomsday Festival, and newbies like Words by Water in Kinsale in October and Write by the Sea in Kilmore Quay in September. No self-respecting town wants to be left out. Many festivals come with short story competitions, and publishing opportunities for emerging writers are better than ever.

Enthusiasm abounds in media coverage, led by the literary pages of *The Irish Times*, home of the Hennessy New Irish Writing Competition, *The Independent* newspaper and the Sunday papers. RTÉ Radio arts programming provides supportive coverage of the literary scene.

New and established literary magazines, such as *The Stinging Fly*, *The Moth* and *Banshee* offer publishing space to new voices all the time, particularly short story writers. Small independent presses such as Tramp Press, The Lilliput Press and New Island Books have shown a knack for discovering outstanding talent.

On the establishment side, there is Aosdána, set up in 1981, a sort of artists' guild with 250 members of whom almost 100 are in the literature category. The affiliation was introduced to honour artists, which is nice, but also support them financially, which is very nice. More than half of the peer-appointed members receive an annual grant, *cnuas*, of €17,180 from the Arts Council to help them 'concentrate their time and energies in the full-time pursuit of their art'. Even the tax authorities are kind to Irish writers. Under the Artists' Exemption scheme, authors do not have to pay tax on revenue earned from artistic works (up to €50,000).

Her story

'I know now that I began writing in a country where the word *woman* and the word *poet* were almost magnetically opposed. One word was used to invoke collective nurture, the other to sketch out self-reflective individualism. Both states were necessary – that much the culture conceded – but they were oil and water and could not be mixed. It became part of my working life, part of my discourse, to see these lives evade and simplify each other. I became used to the flawed space between them. In a certain sense I found my poetic voice by shouting across that distance.'[ix]

These are the words of Eavan Boland, one of Ireland's greatest living poets. For so long, Irish women writers competing directly with men have had to shout across the distance. But something changed at the beginning of the 2010s, at least in terms of media coverage and accolades. Though parity of recognition was and still is elusive, suddenly women were pushing an open door. There is an awful lot of catching up to do, matched by great enthusiasm to do the work. I remember reading the short story anthology *The Long Gaze Back* in 2015 and feeling a rising sense of excitement that I had in my hands precious proof that Irish women had been writing great literature for a long time. A second anthology of Northern Irish writers, *The Glass Shore*, followed in 2016. Alan Hayes' *Reading the Future*, which came out in 2018, was the first anthology of Irish writing to feature more female than male writers.

There is no doubt that a new wave of writers in the past decade have knocked the socks off the critics with their originality and talent. Starting with Emma Donohue's Booker Prize shortlisting for *Room* in 2010, it became normal for a steady stream of new Irish female writing stars to be referred to only in superlatives. In the *New York Times* review of her 2014 debut, *A Girl is a Half-Formed Thing*, Eimear McBride was described as the latest in an illustrious line of Irish typographical reformers.

'Her book forgoes quotation marks and elides verbiage for sense, sound and sheer appearance on the page. For emphasis it occasionally wreaks havoc on capItalS and reverses letter order. It is, in all respects, a heresy — which is to say, Lord above, it's a future classic.'[x]

It seemed as if a powerful correction was taking place before our eyes that finally allowed Irish women a fair share of the limelight and accolades. As a reflection of the mood, to mark International Women's Day 2015, *The Irish Times* produced a poster of Women Writers. The 12 chosen were Maria Edgeworth, Augusta Gregory, Edith Somerville & Violet Martin, Kate O'Brien, Elizabeth Bowen, Molly Keane, Mary Lavin, Maeve Brennan, Edna O'Brien, Jennifer Johnston, Eavan Boland and Anne Enright. One day someone will dare to mix the two sexes.

Among living women writers, confidence and urgency on one side met newsworthiness on the other, giving us long-awaited momentum. As Anne Enright wrote in 2017: 'In the last six years there has been a stream of notable debuts by Irish women, to complement the stream of notable debuts by Irish men. ... They are publishing in a time of cultural change, and into a new awareness, one that is fed by social media, acknowledged in print, supported by publishers and encouraged by festival curators.'[xi]

That stream has continued to flow, a mixture of classic and new forms of story-telling. Some authors, like Sara Baume, Lisa McInerney and Anna Burns, are writing inventive, cutting-edge literary fiction that leaves critics spinning with delight or confusion. Others, like Liz Nugent and Sinead Moriarty, have enjoyed best-selling success writing genre fiction. Leading the way is Marian Keyes, whose first 12 novels sold 35 million copies worldwide.

The creative fever has spread beyond fiction. Books of essays and memoir by Irish women are also appearing in the best-seller charts, as well as being reviewed with what comes close to universal awe. Ruth Fitzmaurice led the way with *I Found My Tribe*, her inspiring account of life with her terminally ill husband and five young children. Since then we have been treated to wonderful, thought-provoking prose in *I Am, I Am, I Am* by Northern Ireland-born Maggie O'Farrell, *Notes to Self* by Emilie Pine and *Constellations* by Sinéad Gleeson.

The inside track

We cannot speak of the success of Irish writers without delving a little into the privilege of our position – in part cultural, in part geographical. A high price was paid for this privilege. When English finally became the dominant language in Ireland in the 19th century, it was an incalculable loss to Irish heritage and identity, our sense of self. But it was a communal loss for which the statute of limitations has passed. It is rarely felt on an individual level any more.

Yet I can trace this loss in my own life. My mother is a native speaker of Irish from the Connemara Gaeltacht. My father was from a family well inside the Pale which had adopted English as early as the 18th century. As someone who was raised bilingual, I still feel that Irish words fit most naturally in my mouth and are closest to the essence of what I am naming. Yet I am now an adult with broken Irish, my early mother tongue having been swamped by English, which is a most formidable opponent.

My Irish atrophied over the years because one of the main drivers of language use is necessity, and I hardly ever really needed it. No surprise that I don't know the word for atrophied in Irish. In becoming a professional writer, my goal was to accumulate as much English as possible, just as my Irish-speaking ancestors in Connemara accumulated as much English as possible for their dealings with officialdom and their likely emigration. They kept both languages going for three generations until, inevitably, the old one was lost in the final scattered generation, mine. The revival of commitment to the Irish language in the past 30 years, seen in the number of Irish-language schools that have been founded as part of a grass-roots movement, is heartening.

But English remains the language of opportunity, most particularly for writers, thanks to the massive market of native and second-language speakers. When the English-language publishing world was divided up between London and New York after the Second World War, the British got the Commonwealth and Ireland. This was no ad hoc arrangement but a result brought home by a British delegation that negotiated with US publishers. This meant that the gatekeepers to the publishing industry for Irish writers were only a hop, skip and a jump away across the Irish Sea.

Irish people had been moving in and out of Britain for generations, gaining familiarity with British society from the bottom up. That expertise was a competitive advantage for writers, even if it wasn't their first-hand experience. Because of the historically unequal relationship between the two peoples, we paid attention to the English. We learned their history, read their books, consumed their entertainment in film and television, followed their news. We had one-way access to a shared cultural space so that we were speaking their language in more ways than one.

As far back as books like the phenomenally successful *Sketches of Irish Character* (1829) by Anna Maria Hall, the English have had an appetite for Irish stories and characters. The smaller neighbour had the advantage of closeness to Britain accompanied by a slight exoticism. When Irish writers talked, the English listened. Today, Irish authors have proportionally better access to the UK publishing scene than citizens living in Commonwealth countries. At the same time, they are championed by Irish publishers in a thriving domestic publishing sector.

Not to forget the global power of the language itself, led by the United States, whose readers historically have a special interest in Ireland. The English dividend is so ubiquitous in every market that its value is hardly noticed by those on the 'right' side of the language flow. Established in 1994, Literature Ireland has funded the translation of 1,900 titles published in Ireland into 56 languages. Writers in other languages are like salmon fighting their way upstream. Only three per cent of all the books published in the US are works in translation. The share has risen to 5 per cent in the UK. According to Three Percent, a resource for international literature at the University of Rochester, only a fraction of the titles that do make their way into English are covered by the mainstream media. 'Despite the quality of these books, most translations go virtually unnoticed and never find their audience.' I invariably find translated works of contemporary Irish writers when browsing in Swiss bookshops. Needless to say, the same does not apply for Swiss authors in Ireland.

A writer has an irrepressible urge not just to record words on the page but to express something meaningful and for that message to be heard. Without the reader, this essential communication about the human condition cannot take place. When the message is powerful enough, it can echo for centuries. The appreciation that Irish writers have received in recent generations has amplified the voice of the nation in a remarkable way and continues to inspire new writers at home and abroad. The canon of contemporary Irish literature confirms that this attention is deserved, and that it matters, as Colm Tóibín's character Mary says in *The Testament of Mary*, 'that the truth should be spoken at least once in the world.'[xii]

Endnotes

[i] http://www.stgallpriscian.ie/index.php?id=7056&an=1 with input from Kuno Meyer's translation

[ii] *Sunday with Miriam*, RTÉ Radio 1, 11.11.2018

[iii] BBC, John Morgan, Report on Censorship in Ireland, 05.04.1965

[iv] Joyce, James, *A Portrait of an Artist as a Young Man*, Wordsworth Editions, 1992, p. 191

[v] 'Anna Burns brings intimacy, insight and laughter back from the beyond to Belfast' by Freya McClements, *The Irish Times*, 16.04.2019

[vi] Foster, R.F., *The Irish Story*, Allen Lane The Penguin Press, 2001, p. 3

[vii] From an interview given by Martin Allioth at *Stimmen aus Irland*, an event which took place in La Capella, Bern, 21.01.2019

[viii] 'Don't be afraid of writing, it's not as hard as it looks,' *Irish Independent*, 01.08.2012

[ix] *Object Lessons, The Life of the Woman and the Poet in Our Times* by Eavan Boland, Carcanet Press Ltd., 1995, p. xi

[x] *New York Times* review by Joshua Cohen, 14.09.2014

[xi] *London Review of Books*, Vol. 39, No. 18, pp 33-35, 21.09.2017

[xii] *The Testament of Mary: A Novel* by Colm Tóibín, Simon & Schuster, 2012, p.67

CHAPTER 5

The Irish are Catholic

The accumulation of wealth has always been a significant side effect of the activities of the Roman Catholic Church in Ireland. Today, the country's 26 dioceses and 160-odd religious orders of elderly men and women sit on a multibillion-euro land and property portfolio. But are they sitting comfortably?

The primary asset of the Church is not money but souls, and Ireland could always be counted on to supply its share of the faithful. Not just quantity but quality: Ireland produced devout, obedient Catholics and was long cherished by the Vatican as the last remaining stronghold of true Catholicism in the Western world.

Until now.

At the turn of this century, a significant demographic shift took place. For the first time since the foundation of the Irish State, the percentage of the population declaring to be Catholic fell below 90 per cent[i]. And now that the leak has sprung, there seems to be no way of stemming the flow. The latest census figures (2016) put the share of Catholics at 78 per cent, with one in ten people now ticking the 'no religion' box.

Are the Irish Catholic? Like metamorphic rock, the fusing of Catholic and Irish identity was produced by great heat and pressure over a long period of time. But unlike rock, the process appears to be reversible and the reversal is happening in real time.

Throughout my childhood, Catholicism was all-pervasive in

Irish lives, like the weather. It was in our language ('Sweet Mother of Divine!'), in our diet, our home décor, in our parents' sex lives, in our most private thoughts on the way to Confession. Since then, the Catholic imprint on daily life has faded, crowded out by other cultural influences and fervent consumerism. Feck suffering and waiting for the afterlife, the Irish now want their heavenly rewards here on earth. While the Church still wields significant influence, especially in education, there has been a collective turning away from much of what the institution stands for.

The Catholic Church in Ireland held its flock in a tight embrace for generations. Working in step with the State, it had a quasi totalitarian reach over the lives of individuals. The priests were the most important community leaders in every parish. The poorer or more devout the family, the greater the priest's power over them. On a local level, the priest's word could send a child into care, keep a woman in an abusive relationship, cost a teacher his or her job. From schooling to healthcare, from birth to death and every major life event in between, nothing happened without the involvement of the Church. On a national level, public representatives only voted for legislation that would be acceptable to their bishops, sometimes with direct intervention behind the scenes from the latter. Government ministers had a deferential relationship with the hierarchy and toed the Church line on censorship and all legal matters relating to sexual relationships and reproduction. The dominant position of the Catholic Church meant the nation's small Protestant minority lived under the same strictures, only without the guilt.

Religion	2011	2016
Catholic	84.2%	78.3%
No Religion	5.9%	9.8%
Church of Ireland	2.9%	2.8%
Muslim	1.1%	1.3%
Orthodox	1%	1.3%
Presbyterian	0.5%	0.5%
Other stated religions	2.7%	3.2%
Not stated	1.6%	2.6%

Source: Central Statistics Office

The Protestant minority in the Republic declined in numbers throughout the 20th century through emigration and intermarriage with Catholics. Nevertheless, the community has survived and in fact has grown over the past two decades due to immigration and Catholic converts. Often perceived as a privileged group apart in Irish society or as victims of an oppressive Catholic state, the truth is more multi-layered. Historians Ida Milne and Ian D'Alton explore these layers in a collection of essays they edited, *Protestant and Irish: The minority's search for place in independent Ireland* (2019).

Now a history lecturer at Carlow College, Ida Milne grew up on a farm in County Wexford, one of five children in a Church of Ireland family. The Milnes were firmly embedded in their mixed religion community and had the local GAA pitch on their land. As a child, she took part in the commemoration of the 50th anniversary of the Easter Rising in her national school. She was proud to have the honour, as the youngest in the school, of putting the 1916 Proclamation up on the wall. 'We felt just as Irish as everyone else and didn't see ourselves in any way associated with Britain.'

'My motivation to work on the book was to get rid of that sense of other, the idea that to be Protestant is to be the landlord on the horse. The extremes attract attention but we wanted to show the diversity of Protestant life in Ireland: the tenant farmers, the clerks, the revolutionaries and the GAA players.'

Going through the motions

While, as mentioned, the Protestant community is experiencing a mini-revival through immigration and an influx of Catholic converts, there is no doubt that the country is moving in a secular direction. The change that has taken place in my lifetime is nothing short of revolutionary. The outcome is clear-cut in terms of social policy, as the 2018 abortion and blasphemy votes made abundantly clear, but there is plenty of ambiguity when it comes to social behaviour.

True Catholic believers – people who attend Mass on Sundays and holy days of obligation, confess their sins, take communion regularly and give 'a religious submission of intellect and will'[ii] to Church doctrine – are in the minority. For most Irish Catholics, the Church has become an event management company. Rather than throw out the baby with the bathwater, they have kept the fun stuff, essentially anything that involves dressing up, while completely disregarding the moral dictates of the Church. They might love their neighbour, up to a point, but when it comes to the old taboos of pre-marital sex, contraception, abortion, homosexuality and divorce, people feel free to follow the dictates of their own hearts and circumstances.

This going-through-the-motions arrangement is clearly a transitional phase. We are still dealing with a middle generation (mine) who received a medium dose of Catholicism growing up. Our parents were force-fed a strong dose, but the ones to watch are our children, anyone under 30. Will their watered-down dose of Catholicism be enough to keep them involved, however superficially? Mass attendance figures for younger people, though relatively high in European terms, indicate not.

A little more than half (54 per cent) of Irish people aged 16 to 29 identify as Catholic while 39 per cent of this demographic say they don't belong to any religion or denomination. Of these young Catholics, just one in four attends Mass weekly, apart from special occasions such as weddings and funerals. These were the results of a joint British-French study based on data from the European Social Survey.[iii]

Fewer than 130,000 people attended the open air mass said by Pope Francis in the Phoenix Park in Dublin on August 26th, 2018. An estimated one million people turned out at the same venue in 1979 to see Pope John Paul II, the last pontiff to visit Ireland before Francis.

No-one is more aware of this than the Archbishop of Dublin and Primate of Ireland Diarmuid Martin. In 2017 he gave a speech in St Mary's, Haddington Road, in leafy Dublin 4 that explored where the church would be in 10 years' time. Martin admitted weekly mass attendance was as low as two per cent in some Dublin parishes. With regard to church leadership, he drew a comparison with the youthful Irish government.

'I was struck at the fact that there are more members of the current cabinet under 45 than there are of priests of that age in the diocese. The same applies to leadership cadres in many other sectors of society. The challenge is not just about numbers but also about a generational separation. It is about a separation in which leadership in the formation of many aspects of our culture belongs to one generation and leadership and the mainstream membership of the Church belongs to another. How do you bridge that gap?'[iv]

Not without a magic wand. In an earlier address, Martin described the current phase as the most difficult for the Church since Catholic Emancipation in 1829.

Although Irish Catholics in the Republic enjoy the privilege of belonging to the dominant religion of their country, in cultural memory they still hold onto their previous identity of being a disadvantaged group. Catholics in Northern Ireland, continued victims of discrimination and injustice until very recent times, have provided a reminder of that alternative destiny.

Bad old days

Before the Reformation (1517 – 1648), the Irish Church had developed its own brand of Christianity which suited the place and the people rather well. The monastic tradition was very strong and many indigenous pagan practices had been absorbed into Christian rituals. The Norman lords (blow-ins of just a couple of centuries) and Gaelic lords shared the native religion and language.

When Queen Elizabeth I took back control of England after Queen Mary's Catholic reign, she tried to impose the English brand of Protestantism next door in Ireland too. But the attempted reform was rejected because the Irish liked neither the message nor the messenger. Elizabeth's successor, James I, took a different approach to turning Ireland Protestant by initiating the

Plantation of Ulster as a way of neutralising the country's most Gaelic province. The settlers who were granted land had to be English-speaking, Protestant and loyal to the king and they were banned from taking Irish tenants.

Inevitably, the colonisation project led to violence which culminated in an Ulster Catholic rebellion in 1641 in which Protestants were massacred and expelled. The rebellion was quashed with fresh atrocities committed against the natives. Oliver Cromwell came over to sort out the rebellious Irish once and for all in 1649. Cromwell was only in Ireland for ten months but his name lives on in infamy, and he remains the most hated Englishman ever to have set foot on the island.

Historian Richard Killeen explains Cromwell's legacy with regard to religious identity:

'He [Cromwell] left behind a mopping-up operation that dragged on until 1652 ... What followed was a massive plantation scheme. Cromwell dispossessed every Catholic landowner in the rich provinces of Munster and Leinster and replaced them with reliable English Protestants, who became the antecedents of the eighteenth-century ascendancy. The dispossessed were to remove to the poorer western province of Connaught ... The Cromwellian land confiscations set the pattern of Irish history for the next 250 years. It is no accident that when Irish nationalism eventually formed, it did so on the basis of Catholic solidarity.'[v]

That solidarity still tugs at the heartstrings today in a culturally Catholic nation. This goes beyond a penchant for frilly First Communion dresses. To some extent, Catholic rituals have become a dual celebration of both Irish and religious identity.

Land confiscation was one major problem for Irish Catholics, but the Penal Laws, a series of Acts introduced in the 17th and 18th centuries to make the religion untenable, reached much further.

Priests became outlaws and Catholic worship was prohibited. Catholics were also banned from owning land, teaching, voting or holding public office. Some converted to Protestantism to avoid these punitive restrictions, but forcing the religion underground made it more precious to most Catholics.

By the end of the 18th century, some of the most severe restrictions had been lifted and Catholic schools were allowed again under certain conditions. But the country's three million Catholics, deemed too ignorant and disloyal to be counted upon, were still banned from sitting in Ireland's Church of Ireland (Anglican)-only parliament.

Brothers in arms

Inspired by the egalitarian ideas of the American and French Revolutions, the United Irishmen organisation formed in 1791 with the aim of forging a political union between Catholics and Protestants to reform the Irish parliament from which Catholics and Presbyterians were banned. The United Irishmen felt that Ireland was economically and socially disadvantaged in its relationship with Great Britain and that a more representative government could better defend the country's interests.

Theobald Wolfe Tone, founder of the United Irishmen, wanted to abolish 'the odious distinction between Protestant, and Presbyterian, and Catholic'. His dream was to see 'the three great sects blended together, under the common and sacred title of Irishman'.[vi]

After a few short years, optimism faded in the face of intransigence and the United Irishmen became revolutionary republicans, finally leading a revolt in 1798 that was defeated. In the wake of the rebellion, Westminster took direct control of Ireland with the 1801 Act of Union. The doors were closed on the

Irish parliament for good. There would be no common or sacred title of Irishman that ignored religious affiliation. Instead, in the future lay partition, with a Catholic majority in the Republic, and a Protestant one in Northern Ireland, loyal to the United Kingdom.

The charismatic political leader Daniel O'Connell took up the baton in the 19th century for the rights of Catholics, founding the Catholic Association in 1823 to campaign for Catholic Emancipation, essentially the repeal of the remaining Penal Laws. The Association drew on massive popular support and was largely funded by the Catholic Rent, a subscription of a penny a month. Described by Killeen as 'the first populist, mass mobilization of an entire people in European history, ... the Association created a national network of local committees and activists by tapping into the one existing organizational structure that was tailor-made for the purpose: the Catholic parish system.'

Priests campaigned for the association from the pulpit. There was a powerful confluence of related needs and aspirations. The funds were used to support peasants boycotting absentee landlords or those evicted for their involvement with the organisation. The Association was also able to fund campaigns of Catholic candidates for parliament.

With Irish Catholic MPs being elected to parliament but unable to take up their seats in Westminster because of their religion, the British government had no choice but to bow to the pressure and logic of the campaign by voting through repeal in 1829.

But the systemic injustices and inequalities suffered by Irish Catholics would take much longer to remove and the horror of the Great Famine (1845 – 1848) was around the corner. Long after Catholic Emancipation, the collective memory of dispossession and discrimination among Catholics formed a rich seam for the nationalist cause.

Daniel O'Connell can be thanked for bringing the Catholic Church into politics in the 19th century. But the Irish Church was consolidating power in other ways at the same time, and this development was fostered by the British.

A state within a state

We tend to see the dominating influence of the Catholic Church on Irish politics and society as a feature of self-government, post 1922, as if the Church had moved into the vacuum left by the British. In fact, the power base of the Catholic Church was already well established under British rule and the Church-State partnership was inherited by the new administration. Historically, there had been a fear across the water that the impoverished Irish would swamp British towns and cities. This was already happening to some extent as the Irish poor travelled in search of work. Successive British governments judged it expedient to allow the Catholic Church far-reaching control over its flock. The provision of education, health and welfare increasingly became the preserve of the Catholic Church, with a smaller parallel network operated by the Church of Ireland to look after their own.

Political scientist and historian Tom Garvin describes the partnership inherited by the fledgling Irish democracy in 1918-1922 in stark terms:

'Perhaps the most pervasive legacy of British government in Ireland was the partnership that had developed between the Catholic Church and the British State, giving to the religious organisations the tasks of educating the young, running much of the health system and controlling much of the civic life of the society... In effect this made the Catholic Church in independent Ireland a powerful and autonomous agency which for many purposes operated like a second government or a state within a state. In the areas of health, education and much of public ideological discourse, the power of the Church was enormous. Above all, the Church attempted to control, some would say enslave, much of the intellectual and emotional life of the entire country.'[vii]

Veterans of the same school benches, the Catholic hierarchy and the elites of the new State were natural allies. In forging a new identity, the Free State, buzzing with national pride, sought to be the negative to the United Kingdom. What they are, we are not. They are English speakers, so we will endeavour not to be. They are Protestant so we will cling to the Catholic faith. They play soccer and rugby, so we will raise up our own national sports until they are more beloved. They have loose morals, we will be pure.

Censorship is a perfect example. In 1926, the Minister for Justice, Kevin O'Higgins, created the Committee on Evil Literature to address the concerns of various groups including the Catholic Truth Society and the Irish Vigilance Association, fearful of indecent literature, in particular English publications.

The 1929 Censorship of Publications Act gave the censorship board carte blanche to ban anything remotely questionable. Dr William O'Brien of the DLR Lexicon library explained in an exhibition he curated in 2018: 'It took very little to have a book banned, the merest hint of homosexuality, promiscuity or prostitution was enough. All too often a ban might even rest on only a sentence or a phrase.'[viii] The board did not have to give a reason.

The Register of Prohibited Publications eventually included ten Nobel Laureates: Samuel Beckett, Heinrich Böll, William Faulkner, Anatole France, Harry Sinclair Lewis, Ernest Hemmingway, Thomas Mann, George Bernard Shaw, Mikhail Sholokhov and John Steinbeck.

But the hardest hit were contemporary Irish writers, deprived of sales and cut off from their natural readership. Among them were Lee Dunne, Nora Hoult, Benedict Kiely, John McGahern, Edna O'Brien, Frank O'Connor, Seán Ó Faoláin and Liam O'Flaherty. Meanwhile, Irish readers were deprived of literary treasures and a necessary mirror for their own society.

Edna O'Brien became one of the most banned writers of the 1960s with her novels that dealt frankly with female sexuality. Between 1960 and 1966, she had to endure five of her books being banned, including *The Country Girls* trilogy.

John McGahern's 1965 novel, *The Dark*, was banned for its use of swear words and depictions of a boy masturbating. He lost his job as a primary school teacher in the scandal that ensued. A new Censorship Act in 1967 relaxed restrictions but heavy-handed censorship of taboo subjects, such as abortion, remained a problem for writers and readers up to the 1980s.

The unique position of the Catholic Church was rewarded by special recognition in a subsection of Article 44 of the 1937 Constitution. The document was shown to the hierarchy before it was passed in parliament to make sure that Church and State were singing from the same hymn sheet.

However, at the time, the 'special position' granted to the Catholic Church as 'the guardian of the faith' of the majority was second best for the bishops who had been seeking state religion status for Catholicism. The next subsection of Article 44 recognised the five minority religious denominations in Ireland, including the Jewish faith. Both subsections came to be seen as problematic and were deleted following a referendum in 1972 that garnered 84 per cent support.

A booklet produced for the Mother and Child Scheme. The scheme was never implemented because of joint opposition from the Catholic Church and the medical lobby, which regarded the service as 'socialised medicine', and feared a potential loss of income.

It's a sin

If the Catholic Church had a weak spot in the 20th century it was its inordinate focus on sexual morality. Sometimes the results were ludicrous, more often they were tragic.

Concerned about all-night dancing and immorality, the bishops campaigned to bring in the Dance Hall Act in the 1930s so that priests could have better control of community gatherings. In the 1950s, the bishops brought down a proposed national maternal healthcare scheme because they wanted to prevent mothers from coming across information about contraception at any cost, arguably including the cost of babies' lives. Unmarried women who became pregnant were denounced from the pulpit and risked being interned as unpaid labourers in Magdalene laundries.

When the Irish women's movement emerged in the late 1960s and 1970s, partly in response to stimulus from the United Nations and European Economic Community, activists became by definition adversaries of Church influence. It was no surprise that they identified an organisation run by celibate men with a punitive, controlling approach to female fertility as harmful to women's rights and wellbeing.

They lived in a country where doctors in some Catholic-run hospitals preferred to break a woman's pelvis during labour rather than perform a Caesarean section for ideological rather than medical reasons. They lived in a country where unmarried mothers were bullied into adoption, and birth certificates were forged to hide children's true identity. They lived in a country where married women were expected to have big families regardless of whether they could manage physically, emotionally or financially.

An unlikely ally for the women's movement emerged from another male-dominated, elite institution – the judiciary. From the mid-1960s in particular, the Irish and American Supreme Courts both developed a similar concept of 'unenumerated rights'. From the written text, judges extrapolated rights that were implied rather than written down.

The Irish case of McGee versus the Attorney General in 1973 was a shock to the Church and body politic. Twenty-seven-year-old Mary McGee already had four children and was told that another pregnancy would put her life in danger. She tried to import a spermicidal jelly for her personal use but the package was stopped by customs and she received a letter telling her so. Under the 1935 Criminal Law Amendment Act, it was unlawful to 'sell, expose, offer, advertise ... or import ... contraceptives'. On the grounds of her right to marital privacy, McGee took a case which ended up in the Supreme Court.

Speaking to *The Irish Times* 40 years later, McGee recalled her reaction.

'I just thought "no way, I have to do something about this", not realising the enormity of what I was taking on. I think we were all ready for change though. People wanted children but they also wanted a life.'[ix]

The Supreme Court ruled that the McGees had a constitutional right to marital privacy based on Articles 40 and 41. This opened the way for the government to legislate for the sale of contraceptives. Cue six years of bitter debate and deliberate procrastination before the Health and Family Act of 1979 which allowed married couples (only) to purchase birth control on prescription from a doctor. The sale of condoms was not fully liberalised until 1992.

This was just one of many battles in the war being waged between conservative Catholic forces and proponents of a new liberal-secular ethos. The Catholic lobby won important rounds in the 1980s with the successful introduction of the 8th Amendment to the Constitution (a direct response to the fear of constitutional rights being too broadly interpreted by the judiciary), effectively banning abortion in all circumstances, and the defeat of the 1986 Divorce Referendum. (For more on the 8th Amendment, see **Chapter 7: Irish Women are a Force to be Reckoned With**.)

Suffer little children

In the end, the hegemony of the Catholic Church was broken not from without but from within. The Church had built an empire in health, welfare and education – spheres in which its rank and file had absolute power. And we know what happens with absolute power.

That the Irish Catholic Church and religious orders are today associated with the sexual, physical and emotional abuse of children and vulnerable women is entirely self-inflicted damage. And it is not just because these crimes happened under the Church's authority on a large scale. It is also because, when it came down to it, the people who had so ardently taught us to say mea culpa were not capable of saying it themselves. After so many years of obsession with sexual morality, that double betrayal – the abuse itself and the denials and cover-ups that followed it – was devastating to a relationship already under strain.

The turning away had already begun in a population that was automatically becoming more secular thanks to education, disposable income, television, media, internet and travel. Archbishop Martin recognised this in a speech he gave in 2011.[x]

'The cultural infrastructure which for decades supported belief and the transmission of the faith began slowly to show signs of wear and tear, but we failed to realise just how widespread the damage to that structure had become. People began to drift away from Church practice. For many, the recent sexual abuse scandals – and the mismanagement of the response to them – were the final disillusionment with the Church, and from indifference they moved to anger at the Church.'

Anger, I don't deny my own. I wasn't greatly bothered by the hypocrisy of Bishop Eamon Casey and Michael O'Cleary, two church celebrities in my youth, who preached conservative sexual morals while denying the children they had fathered. These men were exposed in Irish newspapers in the early 1990s, the beginning of a whirlwind of scandal that engulfed the Church. The crimes which were subsequently revealed proved to be a lot less forgivable than breaking vows of celibacy and denying paternity. (It has since emerged that three women made allegations that they were sexually abused as children by Casey. Two of the women received compensation payments from the Church.)

So while I didn't care about those failed fathers living a lie, I did care about the suffering of innocents. This was a moment in Irish history when the media in the UK and Ireland played a crucial role in shining a light into dark places. They brought us heart-breaking stories that were impossible to ignore.

The Irish public became aware of the stomach-turning litany of horrors not just through news reports but most effectively through documentaries in the mid-1990s, beginning with *Suffer Little Children* in 1994 by Chris Moore on UTV. This documentary detailed the appalling career of the paedophile priest Brendan Smyth who raped and assaulted more than 140 children over a 40-year period, facilitated by the superiors in his order who moved him from parish to parish in Dublin, Belfast and the United States despite knowing he presented a danger to children. *Dear Daughter* in 1996 brought us the tragic early life of Christine Buckley in Goldenbridge orphanage. *Sex in a Cold Climate* was a 1998 documentary about the mistreatment of Irish women and girls in Magdalene laundries. Mary Raftery's *States of Fear* documentaries on RTÉ television in 1999 lifted the lid on widespread abuse in residential industrial schools. In 2002 she made *Cardinal Secrets* about how the Dublin diocese handled allegations of abuse by priests in its parishes. This led to the archdiocese setting up its own commission of investigation under Judge Yvonne Murphy.

It took another documentary, this time the BBC's *Suing the Pope* in 2002 about Father Seán Fortune, another notorious sex offender, in this case in the diocese of Ferns, for the government to set up the first State inquiry into clerical sex abuse. The Ferns Report in 2005 was added to the pile, followed by the Cloyne Report in 2011 on sexual abuse in the diocese of Cloyne. Time and again, investigators found an institutional mindset that placed protecting the institution above protecting the victim. Dangerous priests were knowingly sent into direct contact with children, with all the power and prestige of their position intact.

It was very difficult to listen to all these revelations of cruelty and negligence, to hear the stories of pain, lives destroyed, suicides and not to emerge with feelings of cynicism or outright loathing for the organisation that showed such a brazen disregard for the safety of children. For many, the brand was contaminated for good.

The response of then Taoiseach Enda Kenny to the Cloyne report in a speech he made to the Dáil shows that this repugnance was shared by the political leadership, even a self-described faithful Catholic like Kenny. Referring to the attempt of the Holy See to frustrate the inquiry in 2008, Kenny lambasted the Church authorities:

'... the Cloyne Report excavates the dysfunction, the disconnection, the elitism that dominate the culture of the Vatican to this day. ... The rape and torture of children were downplayed or "managed" to uphold instead, the primacy of the institution, its power, standing and "reputation".' [xi]

This is not Rome, Kenny declared, this is the Republic of Ireland.

'A Republic of laws, of rights and responsibilities, of proper civic order, where the delinquency and arrogance of a particular version, of a particular kind of "morality" will no longer be tolerated or ignored.'

A new paradigm

In effect, Ireland had its own iron curtain behind which the Church managed to preserve a kind of moral and cultural isolationism that echoed the political and cultural isolationism of Communist countries in the same era. Many ordinary people were protected and looked after under both these systems. Today, they may look back with nostalgia to a time when they received practical support and had a direction in life. They had the comfort of certainty and of knowing what to think. And they had the choice to turn a blind eye to those who fell foul of the system, reassured that their own faith and obedience would ensure their immunity from misfortune. (One key difference between Communism and Irish Catholicism was that emigration was always an option for dissenters in Ireland.)

For a long time, the people of Ireland lived a very plain existence, and the Church was their only exposure to a wider, more magnificent world. As John McGahern wrote in his 2005 autobiography, *Memoir*:

'The church ceremonies always gave me pleasure, and I miss them even now. In an impoverished time they were my first introduction to an indoor beauty, of luxury and ornament, ceremony and sacrament and mystery.'[xii]

But this plain existence, despite how much it was romanticised by political leaders at the expense of Ireland's economic development, was not to last. And when prosperity came in by the front door in the 1960s, fear left by the back door, leaving the Church without its most important instrument of control. Mary McGee certainly wasn't afraid when she took her contraception case.

Powerful factors combined in the 1960s to accelerate change, including the advent of television and the introduction of a new economic policy favouring foreign investment. Free secondary education (opposed by the Church) and new job opportunities took away the attraction of an education gained by joining a religious community, and vocation numbers began to shrink, freefalling to the current low of fewer than ten priests per year nationally[xiii].

In a country that decriminalised homosexuality and opened its arms to women presidents a generation ago, the celibacy rule and the ban on women priests seriously undermine the Church's ability to connect with the new type of ordinary person.

If the Church and State are no longer singing from the same hymn sheet, the old partnership is no longer sustainable. A new paradigm is needed. Attention is now turning to the old battlefronts in the struggle against Catholic power: healthcare and education. And the chorus of discontent is getting louder. The momentum for schools and hospitals to be transferred to full State control is noticeable though the pathway to achieve this final true separation of Church and State is bound to be costly and complicated.

When the bishops' conference came out with a new set of guidelines for Catholic hospitals in July 2018, the Taoiseach Leo Varadkar accepted their right to do so but noted that he expected the guidelines of the medical council to be followed in publicly funded hospitals. 'We need to work out a process and a system over the next couple of years when it comes to both health and education to make sure that the approach is one that is more appropriate for a modern country,' Varadkar said.

The prospect of Irish women being turned away from State-funded hospitals when seeking health services that are legal here is no longer tenable. The country's 20 Catholic hospitals[xiv] have traditionally refused to perform sterilisations, for example, a position tolerated by the health service. But a new generation of leaders has no intention of allowing this exceptionalism to continue with regard to abortion services post repeal.

The problem in education centres on State-funded primary

schools. Ninety per cent of all pupils in Ireland's 3,300 State primary schools attend Catholic-run schools, while 5.7 per cent are enrolled in multi-denominational schools. The rest attend schools run by other denominations (a right which is dearly cherished by religious minorities including Protestants and Muslims). According to Department of Education figures for 2018, the multi-denominational sector, represented by 119 primary schools, is growing steadily, while enrolment in Catholic schools stagnates. The same shift is taking place at post-primary level where 45 per cent of students attend multi-denominational schools (349 in total).[xv]

The lifting of the so-called baptism barrier in 2018, under which over-subscribed Catholic primary schools were prioritising baptised children over children of other religions or none, is a significant move.

The scenario of 'no baptism certificate, no place' was worrying at many levels, even if it only happened in a minority of schools. In his May 2018 reform of education legislation, then minister for education, Richard Bruton, singled out this problem as worth addressing, stating, 'Parents should not feel pressured to baptise their child to get access to their local school'.[xvi] The latest reform can be seen as the opening salvo in a longer-term campaign to curtail the religious nature of these schools.

Catholic schools welcome all comers, in normal circumstances. But with only half of marriages taking place in a Catholic Church, there is increasingly a mismatch between what families want and what is available. Outside the larger population centres, parents who want their children educated locally often have no choice but to send them to a school run with a Catholic ethos because there are no other options in their community.

While many see Catholic schools as too influenced by religion, some complain they are not Catholic enough. Conservative Catholics, or those who claim to represent them, long for more control and the means to create a purely Catholic space where their children can be educated about sexuality and moral values according to their parents' wishes. Speaking on RTÉ Radio on February 4, 2019, Maria Steen of the Iona Institute complained about Catholic schools being the default provider for everyone.

'It seems to me that the State is determined to make the educated Catholic a dying breed. The partnership model of State and Church education is broken. We have seen over the last number of years an open bias and hostility towards religious education in general and Catholic education in particular.'

There is no doubt that healthcare and education are the two areas to watch in the next decade. The new Ireland that has emerged in the last 20 to 30 years has repeated the reflex of the Free State a century ago, which was to reject the old masters. Before, we were defined by rejecting the British way, now we are defining ourselves by rejecting the Catholic way. This development is taking place among a wider regional shift towards a post-Christian Europe. We know what we are no longer about. But do we know what we are about? That's what we need to figure out.

In focus: True believer

Galway-born Father Conor McDonogh was ordained as a Dominican priest in 2015.

What was your early experience of Catholicism?

I had a totally ordinary childhood, no stricter than any of my friends but I'd say it was probably more integrally Catholic in the sense that our home life was permeated with references to God. And we would pray at home and so on. My parents had books about all aspects of the faith so that when I had questions, I would just turn to the books. And we had the internet and I would go on Catholic websites and ask my questions. Because I had huge questions, loads of doubts.

As a new priest, what is your experience of the Irish Church today?
For young guys coming in, it's a real challenge. In Ireland, people of faith feel quite alienated from the mainstream. The clerical culture is depressed and shell-shocked and still fairly dysfunctional, and yet you have extraordinary, small groups of lay people who are still faithful. The unseen story in the Irish Church is the fidelity of the lay people despite all the scandals. I'm blown away by that again and again.

It is true that many people have drifted away and no longer describe themselves as religious but I'd say a lot of people are still somehow emotionally connected to the Church. I see this at weddings and funerals. Many Irish people who've lapsed would love not to be and they would love to be given compelling reasons to come back, and a healthy community to come back to and they just don't see it. That's what I'm getting from an awful lot of people.

Where do you think the Church will go from here?
I think things will get a lot smaller and the next big challenge will be downsizing in a positive way, letting go of institutions and so on. I think everyone recognises that divesting from schools and closing down churches just has to happen, even if they are afraid to talk about it. And the question is whether that is giving in to decay or the start of something new.

Beginning this process means recognising that the people are no longer with us and the State is no longer a happy partner for the Church. That's another unusual feature of Irish Catholicism, integralism, where we just thought the State was a co-worker of the Church. There's all that divorce that needs to happen between the State and the Church in broader Irish society, taking account of the smaller number of people who actually believe.

Where does that leave you?

On the one hand, there is a sadness for those who have lost the faith. You're still talking about individuals and as a priest I would love if they had a living relationship with Christ and felt at home in the Church. Every person who's not feeling that way is a tragedy for me. At the same time, the idea of downsizing is about recognising what's already happened, especially in relation to schools and so on.

Part of the problem is that an older generation of priests just can't bring themselves to admit what has happened and how far things have gone. They still have the mindset that basically everyone who lives in the parish boundaries is a parishioner. They still think that a Catholic education is for everyone. But it's not. There are plenty of people who would reject what a Catholic education has to offer and we have to be OK with that and say that we need to be part of a more diverse offering.

The fear for younger Catholics, the minority who really believe and would sign up to all the Church's teachings, is that the necessary change won't happen and the Church will lose its way. If this older generation allows all the Catholic institutions just to drift vaguely in the direction of secularity rather than actually being willing to go through the divorce, it will make it harder for us to start building again.

Endnotes

[i] https://www.cso.ie/en/releasesandpublications/ep/p-cp8iter/p8iter/p8rrc/

[ii] https://w2.vatican.va/content/john-paul-ii/en/motu_proprio/documents/hf_jp-ii_motu-proprio_30061998_ad-tuendam-fidem.pdf

[iii] https://www.stmarys.ac.uk/research/centres/benedict-xvi/docs/2018-mar-europe-young-people-report-eng.pdf St Mary's University and the Institut Catholique de Paris using data from the European Social Survey, Europe's Young Adults and Religion

[iv] https://www.dublindiocese.ie/the-church-in-dublin-in-10-years-time/

[v] Killeen, Richard: *Ireland: 1000 things you need to know*, Atlantic Books London, 2017, p.47

[vi] http://www.irishphilosophy.com/2013/06/20/wolfe-tone/

[vii] Garvin, Tom: *Preventing the Future: Why was Ireland so poor for so long?*, Gill Books, 2005, p.3

[viii] DLR Lexicon 2018 Exhibition curated by Dr William O'Brien

[ix] 'Anniversary of family planning case brings a sense of déjà vu' by Carol Ryan, *The Irish Times*, 07.05.2013

[x] Finance Area Meetings Address. Reflections on the recent meetings on pastoral planning and financial support in the Archdiocese of Dublin, 12.12.2011 (location not given), speech on dublindiocese.ie

[xi] Enda Kenny's speech to the Dáil following Cloyne report, RTÉ News, 20.07 2011

[xii] McGahern, John, *Memoir*, Faber & Faber, p.201

[xiii] https://www.irishexaminer.com/ireland/special-report--diocese-by-diocese-the-state-of-the-catholic-church-on-the-island-of-ireland-today-469022.html

[xiv] https://www.thetimes.co.uk/article/7f6edc3c-8f7f-11e8-8c1a-b63727488402

[xv] Department of Education and Skills, 'Preliminary enrolments in primary and post-primary schools Press Release, 27.12.2018

[xvi] https://www.education.ie/en/Press-Events/Press-Releases/2018-press-releases/PR18-05-09.html

CHAPTER 6

The Irish want a United Ireland

'It is the firm will of the Irish Nation, in harmony and friendship, to unite all the people who share the territory of the island of Ireland, in all the diversity of their identities and traditions, recognising that a united Ireland shall be brought about only by peaceful means with the consent of a majority of the people, democratically expressed, in both jurisdictions in the island.'

Article 3 of the Constitution of Ireland
(excerpt, amended 1998)

'The British Government has no selfish or strategic or economic interest in Northern Ireland: our role is to help, enable and encourage. Britain's purpose...is not to occupy, oppress or exploit but to ensure democratic debate and free democratic choice. Partition is an acknowledgement of reality, not an assertion of national self-interest.'[i]

Peter Brooke, then Secretary of State for Northern Ireland,
London, 9 November, 1990

Imagine a small company that makes plastic forks. It has always lost money but has survived because it belongs to a big company that produces stainless steel forks. The big company has said more than once that it has no strategic or economic interest in holding onto the plastic fork company.

A few miles away, a medium-sized company that makes plastic knives is keeping a close eye. This company is looking to grow and believes a merger with the plastic fork company would be the best way forward. It hires a plane to fly over the plastic fork company pulling a banner that reads, 'YOU COMPLETE ME'.

But the staff and management of the plastic fork company are split. A narrow majority of the board are firm believers in the fork business. Their fathers and grandfathers made forks and were part of a great fork tradition best represented by the big fork company. They don't like change and they don't trust knife-makers. The rest of the board, well disposed towards plastic knives, argue in vain for a brighter future of plastic forks and knives together under one roof. We're all plastic at the end of the day, they say. No surrender, say the forkmen.

The plastic knife company settles down for a long wait.

*

There is only one reason that Northern Ireland still exists today and it is spelled out in the Good Friday Agreement of 1998. It is because the (mainly Unionist[ii]) majority in Northern Ireland wishes to remain in the union with Great Britain that forms the United Kingdom. According to the Agreement, when that majority looks in doubt, the Secretary of State for Northern Ireland should call a vote on its status, the so-called border poll.

The two external players in the saga, the UK government and the Republic of Ireland, are not on the same page as the Unionists. Officially, the UK is neutral about the fate of the six counties across the water, avowing no selfish interest in maintaining the union, while the Republic of Ireland in theory wants to integrate that final corner of the island, and is just waiting until the time is right.

So the preference of the majority inside Northern Ireland is protected and nothing will change until the majority opinion changes. What could bring about such a change? On the one hand, Northern Irish demographics; on the other hand, developments in the two countries that translate into push or pull factors.

Demographics are important because the Unionist / Nationalist split is broadly a Protestant / Catholic one. When Northern Ireland was created in 1921, the territory had a Protestant majority of 65 per cent. That simple majority is already gone, with the 2011 census recording 48 per cent with a Protestant community background against 45 per cent Catholic. The rest were non-Christian (1 per cent) and non-religious (6 per cent).

The shift is continuing, accompanied by increasing numbers of people not affiliated to any religion. A 2017 labour force survey[iii] showed the religious composition of the working age population as 38 per cent Protestant, 43 per cent Catholic and 18 per cent 'other/non-determined'. In my plastic fork company allegory, I left out this latter important group, people who come from both traditions or neither and are more likely to be influenced by the head than the heart.

The question for the near future is whether Unionist parties will be able to reach outside their traditional Protestant voting base and convey the pro-union message to people from a Catholic background. The Alliance party already occupies the neutral space between the two traditions, contributing to a Northern Irish identity which transcends religion. The party's impressive performance in the 2019 European Parliament elections, in which its candidate Naomi Long took one of Northern Ireland's three seats, shows that they have the potential to play a decisive role in where things go from here.

Team GB

What of other developments unrelated to demographics or domestic party politics? Northern Ireland has a relationship with the rest of the United Kingdom. Like any relationship, it is based on ground rules, or at least shared assumptions. These have been undermined in recent times. Could an unsatisfactory Brexit tip the scales in favour of change?

This isn't exactly the union's finest hour. Although 56 per cent of Northern Irish voters said no to Brexit in 2016, they are being dragged along on this most uncomfortable political journey into the unknown. That blatant democratic deficit, combined with the ongoing political instability in Westminster and the restlessness of Scotland, makes the 'better together' message a harder sell than usual. The European Parliament elections again made clear the wishes of voters in the North, with two thirds of first preference votes going to the two candidates committed to remaining in the European Union.

It is apparent that Northern Ireland has a visibility problem in Britain. For instance, Northern Irish athletes were snubbed when the UK Olympic team was rebranded as 'Team GB' in 1999. Their pleas for a more inclusive and accurate name fell on deaf ears. The majority of Britons (77 per cent) have never crossed the Irish Sea or the North Channel to visit Northern Ireland.[iv] As an Irish tourist or resident in England, you are likely to encounter English people who confuse the Republic and the North, asking questions like, 'is that in the bit we own?' So it is not totally out of character that the special circumstances of Northern Ireland were overlooked in the pro-Brexit campaign, with its 'island nation' rhetoric.

Peter Oborne, former chief political commentator of *The Daily Telegraph*, has an interesting perspective on Brexit because he has seen it from both sides. Initially a strong Brexiteer, Oborne came forward in April 2019 with a public reversal of opinion. Mainly, he felt that Brexit should be abandoned because a sensible Brexit was no longer possible due to political mismanagement. But he was honest enough to list the things he had overlooked in advocating to leave the EU, including the disruption to Northern Ireland. And Scotland. Writing on opendemocracy.net, he said he had failed to see how the EU is 'part of the glue which now holds us together in the United Kingdom'.

'I did not foresee how the popularity of our union in Northern Ireland might weaken, if ease of interchange with the Republic were threatened. Like almost everybody else I underestimated the importance of the Good Friday Agreement. And we've all misunderstood the Irish question, even though it has loomed so large in our history for the last 500 years.'[v]

A 2019 poll carried out by Ipsos MORI in Britain on attitudes towards Northern Ireland makes alarming reading for committed Unionists. Support by British people for Northern Ireland remaining part of the United Kingdom is very low. Asked how they would prefer Northern Ireland to vote if it were to hold a referendum on its future, only 36 per cent of respondents said they would like Northern Ireland to stay in the union while 18 per cent preferred that it should leave and join the Republic. A further 36 per cent said that they did not mind either way, with 9 per cent don't knows.[vi]

Whether Brexit has just brought this indifference into the light or engendered it is hard to say. But it is clear that a dramatic change in the international trading and political status of the UK comes at a potentially high cost for Northern Ireland. Not only does it put peace at risk, it takes away something precious: a third non-contentious identity as citizens of the European Union (or fourth, including Northern Irish as an identity). And it undermines the 'Island Economy'[vii] which has evolved since the advent of the Single Market in 1993.

Way back in 1993, the Joint Business Council, comprising the Irish Business and Employers Confederation (Ibec) and the Confederation of British Industry (CBI), was set up as part of the peace process. Its aim was to promote North-South business co-operation. The council published a report in 2018[viii] highlighting the value of the all-Ireland economy. It described the island as an efficiently functioning 'natural economic zone' of scale which delivers significant economic benefits, involving some 13,000 lorries crossing the border daily.

'Our shared vision is a fully connected all-island market which supports greater prosperity and employment growth through increased flows of people, goods, services, energy and investment,' the report said.

Different voices

As someone who grew up on the east coast 125 kilometres from the border, I am aware that my perspective on Northern Ireland is that of an outsider, and I am cautious not to misread or misrepresent the reality. In the interests of transparency (though I think I have already been pretty transparent in this chapter), I admit that I would like to see a united Ireland. I am encouraged that the subject is currently being discussed in more concrete terms than ever before. The removal of Republican terrorism from the equation has freed moderate nationalists to embrace the aspiration more openly.

Typically for someone of my generation from the South with no family connections in the North, I was never brought there as a child. I first crossed the border at the age of 18 with a college friend from Sligo. It was 1990 and the atmosphere at the high security crossing was tense. This was around the time the IRA had launched proxy bomb attacks at British Army checkpoints. Their method was to seize someone working for the army, tie them into their car loaded with explosives and force them to drive to the checkpoint. One of these bombs, detonated by remote control in Coshquin, County Derry, killed the driver and five soldiers, injuring 27 others. The driver's name was Patsy Gillespie and his wife and children were held hostage during the attack.

On the day we crossed the border, British soldiers boarded our bus and ordered the passengers off. They checked our bags on the side of the road. To my shock, they took one young man away, but nobody said a word.

My Sligo friend had grown up crossing the border on a regular basis. In her part of the country, 'everyone' had relatives in the North. Another incentive for her family to make the trip was to fill up with cheap petrol, and she and her siblings were always excited about the different crisps and chocolate bars they could buy in the North. Nevertheless, the border in her childhood was something to be respected and feared. Going through checkpoints – British army and UVF or IRA – was a heavy price to pay for a normal activity like a Sunday drive to visit cousins.

Before writing this chapter from afar, I wanted to visit the North with the specific purpose of speaking to people from both communities. On the bus journey north from Dublin, I kept my eyes peeled for some sign of the border but I missed it. There is nothing to see anymore, no infrastructure, no personnel. I stepped off the bus at the side of the Europa Hotel in Belfast, famous as Europe's 'most bombed hotel', and tried to get my bearings as quickly as possible. Registering all the little differences, the street markings and signs, car registration plates, the pound coins in my pocket, I had the same feeling I have always had in Northern Ireland: disbelief that I was in a different country.

I had arranged to meet the writer Paul McVeigh, but we hadn't set an exact place and time. I had a little wander and called him from Great Victoria Street, naming the hotel I happened to be standing outside. Ten minutes' later he appeared and we claimed two massive armchairs side-by-side in front of an artificial fireplace in the lobby. Over posh coffee and biscuits, I asked him about things we southerners don't usually bring up because of the awkwardness of the history between us. Paul and I are around the same age and neither of us had any power over any of the events in question, yet we both carry traces of those old feelings related to partition, guilt on my side because 'we' abandoned 'them', and resentment on his side for that abandonment.

Paul's first novel, *The Good Son*, is a coming-of-age story about a boy who grew up, as Paul did, in the deprived, mainly Catholic district of Ardoyne in Belfast, during the worst years of the Troubles. The trauma of the conflict looms large over the characters in the book.

'We were Irish, but the people at the top of my street were British. Belfast was divided into little Irelands and little Britains. They were different territories,' Paul explained. 'As a Northern Irish Catholic you were dispossessed in your home. Your home doesn't belong to you. You are told that this is Britain, and you say, no it's not.'

Back living in the city after many years in London, Paul's feelings about identity have changed. 'Nationality is an accident of birth, yet it determined all your affiliations – music, team, flag, passport. All that is learned. People conceive their nationality as more primal but it's not. It was only when I let go of the concept of nationality that I finally became free.'

Paul touched on the difficulty for Northern Irish people, regardless of background, to feel a sense of belonging to the larger culture. 'When I was young, I saw Dublin as my spiritual home, but when I went there I found a lack of welcoming warmth. There was open disdain and judgement from the Southern Irish who saw us as a violent, backward, war-mongering people.'

On the same trip I visited Laura, a mother-of-two and businesswoman from a working-class Unionist background. She welcomed me into her attractive, terraced red-brick house in East Belfast and texted her older neighbour Greig to come and join us for a chat.

Laura grew up in a firmly Protestant area and is proof of the effectiveness of community initiatives. 'I had no contact with Catholics until my teenage years when I was part of a two-year cross-community programme through my youth club. We went south to Galway and Dublin, and I even went to Boston for three weeks when I was 15. I have maintained friendships from that time.'

She enjoys the mix of cultures and would prefer not to have to choose between them. 'I embrace my Irishness, the culture, the literature, the music. My kids do Irish dancing. But I still love to watch Royal weddings and have a bit of fun with it. I like Wimbledon and I support the Irish rugby team.'

Yet Laura doesn't feel at home in either Dublin or London. 'Both are alien to me. We are a place apart. We're all Paddies to the English. As for a united Ireland, if Brexit takes us out of Europe maybe it's thinkable. But how would a Unionist minority exist inside a united Ireland? I'm not sure.'

Laura believes cheap airline travel had a big impact on many people who had never been able to travel before. 'We saw that people are out there living a life, that there's a different way of doing this. It took us out of our hothouse. Gave us a perspective of a bigger world out there.'

Laura's neighbour Greig arrived, brimming with good-humoured mischief, and in the mood for reminiscing. In his 60s now, he described the gay scene in 1970s Belfast which was 'more extreme, fun and full-on' than Dublin, where he also lived for a while.

From a middle-class Protestant background, Greig worked in clothes shops as a young man and later found work in costume design for the BBC. 'When I worked in Belfast city centre, every day there was some sort of upheaval. We used to tap down the clothes in the shop at closing time to look for incendiaries. I remember one particular bombing on a New Year's Eve. It was raining and stormy, like the end of the world. I saw cranes fall over, and electricity cables bouncing in the rain. A few days later we went back to normal. We cleaned up, life went on.'

While Greig prefers the label of Irish to British when he's abroad, he does not identify fully with either. 'I feel really European. I feel more at home in Lisbon where I've been going for more than 30 years. I see them belonging to a society that is so integrated in every single way. They have a way of living without any barriers. Nobody's questioning anything in Portugal, but Northern Irish society is dysfunctional, still black and white.'

Paul McVeigh was more optimistic, despite the fact that the trauma is still very near the surface for many. 'There has been a diluting of the old fixed positions. People are learning from the younger generation. People enjoyed peace. They are beginning to understand they can have that difference of opinion with their neighbours and just carry on with life.'

If you love something, set it free

The biggest ships in the Irish navy of 8 vessels are its 4 patrol ships of 2,256 tonnes each. The Royal Navy has 74 active ships, including 10 nuclear submarines and 6 guided missile destroyers of 8,500 tonnes each. Its largest vessel is a 65,000-tonne aircraft carrier.

Why am I telling you this? We are not going to war with the UK. Yet until 1998, Ireland claimed a part of UK territory as its own. It might have been an empty and hopeless claim, but it was there in black and white in Articles 2 and 3 of the Irish Constitution from 1937.

One of the main historic turning points in recent Anglo-Irish relations was the day voters in the Republic of Ireland accepted the Nineteenth Amendment to the Constitution by 94 per cent. The referendum on May 22, 1998 was held to fulfil one of the conditions of the peace agreement negotiated in Belfast the month before, the Good Friday Agreement. The Irish people were asked to change Articles 2 and 3 to remove the 'territorial claim' to the North that had been in place since the constitution was written.

The claim in the old Article 2 was unapologetic: 'The national territory consists of the whole island of Ireland, its islands and the territorial seas.' It was backed up by Article 3 which said the Irish state would govern the part of the island in its possession, 'Pending the re-integration of the national territory'.

The referendum replaced this with a totally new Article 2 which came at things from a different angle. It confirmed the birthright of anybody born on the island of Ireland to be part of the Irish nation and Irish citizens.

The new Article 3 replaced the claim to the North with an aspiration for unity. Under the new wording, the 'firm will of the Irish nation' is still to 'unite all the people who share the territory of the island of Ireland', but only by peaceful means and with the consent of a majority on both sides of the border. That consent would be tested by a 'border poll', moved up the agenda as one of the ramifications of Brexit.

At the time, the sacrifice of the old Articles 2 and 3 was very important for the Unionist representatives who helped broker the peace. Ulster Unionist Party leader David Trimble expressed satisfaction that 'the illegal territorial claim' had been removed 'and the South now accepts the legitimacy of Northern Ireland'[ix].

But the aim of a united Ireland was still sitting pretty at the very top of the Irish constitution. The issue remained unfinished business for the South.

The border

The 500-kilometre border that runs from Carlingford Lough to Lough Foyle is not just a line on the map. It has always been contested, and it means different things to different people. For many, north and south, it is a scar that in recent years was finally allowed to heal in a context of mutual acceptance. The fading of that scar allowed people who had been oppressed by it to feel free, and it took away the legitimacy of paramilitaries.

But while partition was experienced as a great wrong by Irish nationalists stranded as a minority in a separate territory on the island of Ireland, it represented validation and security to the Unionist majority. The border kept out the Catholic hordes and kept the larger community in a politically and economically dominant position. It allowed Unionists to live in a state that reflected them, in its flag, its currency, its heroes and its values.

That is why the idea of Brexit and the hardening of the border that would logically accompany it was welcomed by a certain sector of the population in the North represented by the Democratic Unionist Party (DUP). They saw Brexit as a means

David Trimble, John Hume receiving their Nobel Prize.

of thwarting the trend towards integration between Northern Ireland and the Republic. The economic disadvantages matter less to them than the political advantage of setting the two jurisdictions on separate, incompatible paths.

The former British prime minister John Major, who made a significant contribution to the peace process, sees it differently: 'Any border between North and South risks reawakening memories of the worst of days. It is not only a trade barrier but a visible manifestation of us and them. It not only divided communities, it divided minds. Its disappearance was one of the best days.'[x] Speaking in Dublin in December 2018, Major was echoing the language being used by the Irish government and EU leaders on this question.

Ironically, the threat of Brexit has also amplified the voices of people from a Unionist tradition in Northern Ireland for whom a united Ireland is no longer unthinkable. Statements to this effect have been made by all sorts of people, from business leaders to social justice activists to the widow of the North's most infamous Unionist, the late Ian Paisley. The old charge of 'Home Rule is Rome Rule' no longer applies to the South, given the progress of the last 25 years through referendums introducing divorce, gay marriage and legal abortion. The Republic is projecting an image of a modern, dynamic, tolerant society, which has shaken off the grip of the Catholic Church. An RTÉ/TG4 exit poll on the day of the 2019 local and European elections found that 85 per cent of Irish voters were 'delighted' that Ireland has become more liberal in recent years.

This energy is spilling over into Northern Ireland where moderate and progressive sections of the population are hungry for social change. The hashtag #TheNorthIsNext, used by the pro-choice and marriage equality campaigners in the North, is an expression of this momentum. Since the 2018 Irish abortion referendum, arch-conservative Northern Irish politicians can no longer hide behind a similar status quo in the Republic. The fact that women and girls in the North were being prosecuted for procuring abortion pills online more than 50 years after abortion services were introduced in Great Britain looks more cruel and bizarre than ever. Finally, in July 2019, British politicians intervened on a human rights basis, passing a cross-party amendment in the House of Commons compelling the government to decriminalise abortion in Northern Ireland. The amendment was passed by a resounding majority together with an amendment which will see same-sex marriage rights extended to Northern Ireland.

This 'interference' only came about because of the collapse of the Northern Ireland Assembly in January 2017. Created under the Good Friday Agreement, the Assembly in Stormont is the devolved legislature in Northern Ireland. The 90-member Assembly has the power to make laws in a wide range of areas, including housing, employment, education, health, agriculture and the environment. The current stalemate could be seen as the inevitable outcome of the fact that the more hard-line parties – Sinn Féin and the DUP – became electorally stronger after peace. While still drawing their salaries (reduced in 2018 and 2019 from £49,500 to circa £35,888 per year), the Members of the Legislative Assembly (MLAs) have not participated in their own parliament or executive since January 2017, leaving civil servants in a caretaking role with no new policies or legislation. The parties have proved unwilling or unable to put their differences aside and work for the greater good of the people they represent. As long as the Assembly is suspended, Northern Ireland looks like an unviable legislative entity, thanks to its electoral breakdown.

This is the political vacuum in which the young writer Lyra McKee was shot and killed by dissident Republicans during rioting in Derry in April 2019. And in which a car bomb exploded in the same city three months earlier. Politicians from all sides came to Derry to show their solidarity, and later attended McKee's funeral service in Belfast. But, as the priest, Martin Magill, asked in his homily, 'Why in God's name does it take the death of a 29-year-old woman with her whole life in front of her to get us to this point?' He pleaded with the politicians present, who included the leaders of Sinn Féin and the DUP, the Irish President and Taoiseach and the British Prime Minister, to do what they were elected to do.

'All our young people need a life that gives them an aspiration for the future. As our politicians we need you to be working together to make that happen, ... especially for those living in deprived areas, so that they will feel the peace process is working for them as well ... .'[xi]

A bitter pill

Sport has provided a welcome channel for shared enjoyment of an all-Ireland identity, regardless of background. The Gaelic Athletic Association played an important role for the Catholic minority in Northern Ireland, providing a safe space for them to express their Irishness in a 32-county context. The all-Ireland rugby, hockey and cricket teams have also inspired people on both sides of the border with their international success. Do Northern Irish Unionists find themselves joining in at Lansdowne Road, singing 'shoulder to shoulder, we'll answer Ireland's call'?[xii] It is certainly a very catchy tune, specially commissioned by the Irish Rugby Football Union to be used in place of the island's two national anthems, and now popular with a number of 32-county sports.

But sport is sport; the feel-good factor quickly disappears when politics rears its ugly head. What are the other reasons to reject unification?

The religious and civil liberties of Northern Protestants would undoubtedly be protected in a diverse united Ireland, with its constitutional language of consent, harmony and friendship. Despite this notional protection, there is a still an enormous psychological barrier to be overcome for a majority community to transition to a position as a minority. This, accompanied by a tangible loss of Britishness through a change of currency or head of state, for example, would be a bitter pill indeed for some.

Non-political concerns include worries about the practicalities of daily life. Despite sustained economic growth and jobs growth,

The Aviva stadium in Dublin, host of countless Irish rugby matches. The Irish rugby team, like the cricket and hockey teams, represents all 32 counties of Ireland

Ireland's current weak points are in the provision of health and housing.

A shortage of affordable public housing has pushed unprecedented numbers of people into the overpriced and insecure rental sector, from where it is one short step to homelessness. Almost one in five households now live in a privately rented home compared to one in 10 a decade ago, according to the homeless charity Focus Ireland. The average house price in Cork (€214,292 in 2019[xiii]) is 50 per cent higher than prices in Belfast, and prices in Dublin are more than two-and-a-half times higher than in the northern city. Ireland is currently in the middle of a homelessness crisis, with local authorities and voluntary organisations providing emergency accommodation for almost 10,000 people.

Northern Irish residents greatly appreciate the egalitarian National Health Service which makes Ireland's two-tier health system look morally reprehensible. Though the Irish State spends more per capita on healthcare than the UK, the results are unsatisfactory, especially in emergency care, and public participation in the costs is complicated. Some 1.5 million people[xiv] are entitled to a means-tested medical card for free public health care, including free GP visits. In addition, all children under six are entitled to free GP visits. Meanwhile 45 per cent of the population pay for private health insurance for hospital care. The latter group will mostly have to pay for GP care, but they get non-emergency hospital care quicker than public patients and in nicer surroundings. That is not something that people brought up with the NHS can stomach.

These pressures on the health service and housing would also give voters in the Republic of Ireland pause for thought. Northern Ireland has never paid its way, famously costing the United Kingdom an estimated 10 billion pounds a year[xv]. This is not the kind of net fiscal balance that any sensible country would sign up for. But we know that nations don't always do sensible things. Realistically, any future change in the status of Northern Ireland would more than likely involve some sort of settlement between the United Kingdom and the new entity, perhaps even support from the EU or elsewhere. Ireland would not be handed a massive bill overnight.

Finances are important, but the most important consideration in any discussion about a potential united Ireland is the risk to peace. The danger of creating a new disgruntled minority falling back into old paramilitary habits must be avoided at all costs. Remnant Loyalist groups are still operating as criminal gangs in some communities, with their drugs and their guns and their feuds. There are people on both sides, like the killers of Lyra McKee and those who place effigies and posters of Catholics on their bonfires, who still carry murderous hatred in their hearts. The last thing we need is to give them an excuse to express that hatred in acts of violence.

Fools rush in

The dream of a united Ireland has endured south of the border. The RTÉ/TG4 exit poll confirmed the results of other polls in recent times. Two thirds of voters indicated that they would vote in favour of a united Ireland if a referendum was held the next day while 19 per cent said they would vote against. Fifteen per cent of respondents said they did not know or refused to answer the question[xvi]. All the main political parties in the Republic support a united Ireland too.

The challenge for all of us with this sensitive issue is to see beyond pre-conceived ideas linked to an accident of birth. The shape of Ireland was imprinted on my brain when I had to learn the rivers, mountains and bays of the island in national school. There was no border on that map, just like there is no border on the weather forecast map of Ireland on State television. The border came later in my consciousness, with nothing but negative associations. So what? It doesn't belong to me, and it cannot be wished away.

Now is the time to listen to those who do not centre the future of Northern Ireland on their own desires but on the greater good. Voices like the moderate nationalist and peace negotiator Seamus Mallon. In his autobiography *A Shared Home Place*, the very first deputy First Minister of Northern Ireland has urged nationalists to be very cautious with any talk or action in the direction of a united Ireland.

Speaking on RTÉ Radio[xvii], Mallon cautioned against a border poll until steps have been taken to ensure that it would not provoke a violent reaction. He suggested that any border poll should seek a majority from both traditions in the North. A simple 50 per cent plus one would be wrong, he said, creating a resentful minority.

Mallon said that Irish unity was the long-term solution but that it may not be attainable for some time.

'We have got to deal with the Unionists in the way that they didn't deal with us. ... The [Northern Ireland] Executive has to get going again and the [Northern Ireland] Assembly has to get going again and we have to get looking at an arrangement short of a 32-county Ireland, arrangements that the Unionists might be able to have confidence in. I myself would look favourably on a form of confederation.'

For a united Ireland to be viable for all 6.6 million people on the island, it cannot be all take and no give. That also applies to the look and feel of a new Ireland or Irish Confederation. Ideas that have been floated in social media and comment pieces include a new flag and national anthem for Ireland, new public holidays to incorporate Unionist traditions, and reforms to parliament. Another potential gesture of goodwill would be for Ireland to re-join the British Commonwealth.

The words of Irish historian J.J. Lee are just as relevant today as they were back in 1989: 'There can be no permanent civilised solution to the Ulster question within the terms of reference of either triumphalist unionism or triumphalist nationalism.'[xviii]

In focus: Psycho-political atmosphere
An excerpt from the 2018 novel *Milkman* **by Anna Burns**
As regards this psycho-political atmosphere, with its rules of allegiance, of tribal identification, of what was allowed and not allowed, matters didn't stop at 'their names' and at 'our names', at 'us' and 'them', at 'our community' and 'their community', at 'over

the road', 'over the water', and 'over the border'. Other issues had
similar directives attaching as well. There were neutral television
programmes which could hail from 'over the water' or from 'over
the border' and yet be watched by everyone 'this side of the road'
as well as 'that side of the road' without causing disloyalty in either
community. Then there were programmes that could be watched
without treason by one side while hated and detested 'across the
road' on the other side. There were television licence inspectors,
census collectors, civilians working in non-civilian environments
and public servants, all tolerated in one community whilst shot
to death if putting a toe in the other community. There was
food and drink. The right butter. The wrong butter. The tea of
allegiance. The tea of betrayal. There were 'our shops' and 'their
shops'. Placenames. What school you went to. What prayers you
said. What hymns you sang. How you pronounced your 'haitch'
or 'aitch'. Where you went to work. And of course there were bus-
stops. There was the fact that you created a political statement
everywhere you went, and with everything you did, even if you
didn't want to. There was a person's appearance also, because
it was believed that you could tell 'their sort from over the road'
from 'your sort this side of the road' by the very physical form of a
person. There was choice of murals, of traditions, of newspapers,
of anthems, of 'special days', of passport, of coinage, of the police,
of civic powers, of the soldiery, the paramilitary. During the era of
not letting bygones be bygones there was any number of examples
and many nuances of affiliation.'[xix]

Endnotes

---

[i] O'Kane, Eamonn, *Anglo Irish Relations and the Northern Ireland Peace Process: From Exclusion to Inclusion from Contemporary British History* Vol. 18, No. 1, Spring 2004, p.84

[ii] The Unionist tradition includes people in Northern Ireland, usually from a Protestant background, who identity as British, or more British than Irish, and vote for 'Unionist' parties.

[iii] Labour Force Survey Religion Report, 2017, Annual Update January 2019, Northern Ireland Statistics and Research Agency

[iv] Ipsos MORI for Kings College London, published 03.04.2019. Conducted online in February 2019 with 1,084 adults aged 16-75 across Great Britain.

[v] https://www.opendemocracy.net/en/opendemocracyuk/i-was-strong-brexiteer-now-we-must-swallow-our-pride-and-think-again/, 07.04.2019

[vi] Ipsos MORI for Kings College London, published 03.04.2019. Conducted online in February 2019 with 1,084 adults aged 16-75 across Great Britain.

[vii] Term coined by Sir George Quigley, Northern Ireland business leader, in 1992 to refer to the positive economic synergies made possible by the Single Market.

[viii] http://www.ibecengineering.ie/IBEC/Press/PressPublicationsdoclib3.nsf/wvIENNewsByTitle/no-deal-brexit-unthinkable,-says-business-north-and-south-11-10-2018/$file/Business+on+a+Connected+Island+-+Ibec-CBI+Report.pdf

[ix] David Trimble speech to Northern Ireland Forum, 17.04.1998, https://cain.ulster.ac.uk/events/peace/docs/dt17498.htm

[x] Speech given by John Major to the Institute of International and European Affairs, Dublin 11.12.2018, http://www.johnmajorarchive.org.uk/2015-2/sir-john-majors-to-the-institute-of-international-and-european-affairs-11-december-2018/

[xi] Father Martin Magill, St Anne's Cathedral Belfast, 24.04.2019

[xii] *Ireland's Call* by Phil Coulter, 1995

[xiii] Daft.ie

[xiv] Health in Ireland Key Trends 2018, published by the Department of Health

[xv] Estimate of public sector finances in Northern Ireland for the financial years 2012-13 and 2013-14 from the Office for National Statistics (ONS) first Country and Regional Public Sector Finances (CRPSF) publication

[xvi] RTÉ TG4 Exit Polls are based on a survey of a randomly selected sample of 3,016 eligible voters outside 156 polling stations across the country on European and local election day 24.05.2019

[xvii] *Marian Finucane*, RTÉ Radio 1 18.05.19

[xviii] Lee, J.J., *1919-1985 Politics and Society,* Cambridge University Press, 1989, p.685

[xix] *Milkman* by Anna Burns, Faber & Faber, 2018, p. 25

CHAPTER 7

Irish Women are a Force
to be Reckoned With

'And the nominees for the archetypal Irish woman are ...' Three women in the audience, representing three contrasting strands of the feminine in Ireland, feel a flutter of anticipation as the camera zooms in. This is their moment.

The first, dressed in combat fatigues, rises to her feet and gazes, steely-eyed, into the middle distance. Strong and courageous, she comes from a long line of warriors, beginning with Queen Maeve of Connacht. She inherited her entrepreneurial spirit from St. Brigid and her ambition from the 16th-century chieftain Grace O'Malley. She was inspired by Rosie Hackett, co-founder of the Irish Women's Workers Union at the age of 18. She remembers the young civil rights leader and MP, Bernadette Devlin, who slapped the face of the Home Secretary in the House of Commons and survived multiple bullet wounds in an assassination attempt. She is part of a female tribe that has always created things – abbeys, businesses, vaccines, self-help groups, political movements, works of art. Her comrades-in-arms today lead political parties, run schools, manage companies, defend the rights of their disabled children, seek justice against abusers. These women have never been absent from Irish society though their achievements were not always recognised or recorded. In 21st century Ireland they are centre stage.

The next nominee is in a pitiful state. She trembles in her seat and keeps her eyes cast down. Though terribly wronged, she is too frightened to be angry. She is the abused girl, disowned by her family and sent to the Magdalene laundry without an explanation. She is Philomena, the young woman in the Mother and Baby home whose child is taken away to be adopted in America without her consent. She is the dying schoolgirl Ann, going through the pain of childbirth alone as the January cold seeps into her bones. She is Joanne, wrongly accused of murdering two newborn babies, hounded by the police and the judiciary. She is the suicidal teenager Miss X, pregnant from rape, who had to go to the Supreme Court to be allowed to travel to England for an abortion. She is the mother who was forced to carry her baby to term with a fatal foetal abnormality because no doctor in Ireland can help her and she cannot afford the journey to England. She is the 17-year-old in Cork whose thong was shown in court in a rape trial to suggest that she was open to sex. She is the trafficked girl forced into prostitution in a strange land. All cried out, she is every girl and woman whose sexuality and fertility, two central aspects of her person that should be the source of greatest joy, are the source of grief and humiliation instead. Throughout the history of the State, she has been shamed and silenced. She has been on her own for a long time but it seems that finally, finally, the country is on her side.

The third nominee is a character we as a society are a lot more comfortable with: the Irish Mammy. How easy it would be if all women were like this. Poor soul, she is completely out of her element at the awards ceremony and mortified by all the attention. A well-meaning biddy, her main concerns are the weather, food and washing clothes. She is an empty nester, still badgering her children to wear a scarf on a cold day. The Irish Mammy relies heavily on stock phrases and loves a bit of gossip. She is harmless and foolish and cannot be patronised enough.

Hilariously, she is even on Twitter and Facebook (written by a man), doling out unasked-for advice to her adult children and making trite observations. Occasionally, one of her number will be cunning enough and have her own television show or stand-up routine (played by a man, obvs) but most Mammies are fated to languish in the provinces and suburbs guarding the good biscuits and waiting for a chance to hang out the clothes between showers.

The Irish Mammy has come to the fore in popular culture in recent years, prompting this surprise nomination. After all that has been achieved to transform women's lives in the past 50 years, it is rather strange that a character so patently removed from all that progress is making such an impact. Who could imagine her ever needing equal pay, a women's refuge or affordable childcare? This comical matriarch is used to sell books and tea towels while her offspring are encouraged to post funny tales on social media of her typical Mammyish behaviour. Happy as long as she can watch her favourite soaps, the Irish Mammy doesn't seem to mind that her identity has been reduced to one thing and that she is being ridiculed for how she lives that role. Accustomed to putting others first, her catchphrase is 'don't mind me'.

So, who is going to win? The feisty, oppressed or frumpy Irishwoman? We will have to consider the women we know and put it to a public vote. And we will have to consider the country they come from and how certain central experiences have shaped Irish women alive today.

A year to remember

The day I was born my mother was supposed to go to work. It was two weeks before Christmas and she was hoping to continue teaching until the school holidays. But events took a different turn at breakfast and my parents rushed to hospital, leaving my

15-month-old sister (about to lose her 'baby' title for good) with the childminder. The story my father used to enjoy telling was that he was still smoking his first cigarette in the waiting room when the matron appeared carrying the bundle who was me, a second girl for my delighted parents.

I enjoyed hearing this story too over the years. And I used to think of everything happening in faded colour, like the photos in our family album, and it all taking place in a happy, more innocent time. Later, I realised the time was not innocent at all, and that many children had sad birth stories, ones they would never get to hear about.

I was one of 67,551 babies born in Ireland in 1971[i], a time when the fertility rate was still very high at 3.93 children per woman, double the rate we have today. Such was the taboo around sex and sexuality that most girls grew up in an information vacuum, ending up with a large family or a child out of wedlock not through choice but rather through lack of information and lack of access to contraceptives. It was illegal to import or sell contraceptives in the country and hospitals did not offer sterilisations.

But with a sexual revolution in full swing in the rest of the English-speaking world, the mission of keeping Ireland an oasis of ignorance and repressive control was becoming untenable. Change was in the air. This was the year when some of the first tactical moves were made in the battle to wrest control of women's fertility from the Catholic Church which effectively dictated the law. The opponents to change were formidable. With just 4 women TDs out of 158 in the Dáil, the body politic was far removed from the lived experience of the female body. In February of 1971, the Catholic Primate of Ireland John Charles McQuaid used the opportunity of his Lenten pastoral letter to remind the faithful, in case there was any doubt, that 'civil divorce is evil and contraception is evil; there cannot be, on the part of any person, a right to what is evil'.

Meanwhile, Mary Robinson, senator and legal advisor to the newly-formed Irish Women's Liberation Movement (IWLM), who would become Ireland's first female president in the hard-fought future of 1990, was drafting a bill for the Seanad to legalise contraception. Robinson needed just 6 senators to get the bill introduced but could not muster the numbers out of a total of 60 members of the upper chamber. In the end, Ireland would have to wait until 1979 for some measure of progress on this front, a bill which allowed access to contraception for married couples on prescription only. That change was forced by a landmark case in the Supreme Court in which Mary McGee won the right to procure contraceptives on the basis of the right to privacy within marriage (see **Chapter 5: The Irish are Catholic**).

Power on one side was met with grit and imagination on the other. In May 1971, IWLM campaigners organised the legendary Contraceptive Train to Belfast, a highly successful publicity stunt. To expose the folly of the Irish ban, campaigners returned to Dublin brandishing contraband contraceptives from the North for the cameras.

Far from the celebratory atmosphere my family enjoyed at the time of my birth, there were 1,842 babies born in 1971 who were recorded as 'illegitimate'. In a conservative, judgmental society, these pregnancies were to all intents and purposes a disaster. If the father would not or could not help, the woman or girl was completely dependent on her family. Even working women found single parenting impossibly daunting at a time when women earned 55 per cent of men's wages[ii] and there was no right to return to work after maternity leave. Traditionally, the most common response by families was to make the problem

The Train, a musical written by Bill Whelan and Arthur Riordan, is a fictional celebration of the actual events surrounding the legendary Contraceptive Train of 1971.

disappear, with or without the expectant mother's consent. She was sent to a religious run, State-funded Mother and Baby home and the baby was adopted or kept in an institution, never to be spoken about again.

Adoption is not an injustice, but forced adoption is a terrible trauma to inflict on a new mother. Sadly, forced adoption was common practice in Ireland up to the 1970s, with a harsh, sophisticated and, in some cases, illegal apparatus in place to keep it up and running. And working hard to keep these babies away from their birth mothers at all costs was the unholy trinity of family, church and state.

The cooperation of the expectant mother's family was the first requirement. The Churches, both Catholic on a major scale and Protestant on a minor scale, proportional to share of population, cooperated not just by being the service provider of maternity care, adoption and residential care but the manufacturers of copious quantities of shame and censure needed to intimidate unmarried mothers, work that started long before conception took place.

The State kept the laws in line with the teachings of the Catholic Church, providing no social welfare safety net for unmarried mothers and blocking access to contraception or abortion. It handed over responsibility for the care and welfare of mothers and babies in crisis pregnancies to the Churches with little oversight. Only a small minority of single mothers were strong enough to resist the pressure and keep their babies. Some of these women went on to found Cherish, the first self-help group for single mothers, in 1972.

The Natural Parents Network of Ireland (NPNI), a group that campaigns for women whose babies were adopted, estimates that more than 100,000 children were separated from their parents through adoption and fostering since the foundation of the State.

'Of these, 42,000 were adopted after the introduction of legal adoption in 1952, and a further number were illegally registered as if born to their adoptive parents (known as "de facto" adoptions).'[iii]

Horrific revelations in 2014 that the remains of up to 800 children were found improperly buried on the grounds of the former Bon Secours Mother and Baby home in Tuam, County Galway made national and international headlines. The government established a Mother and Baby Homes Commission of Investigation[iv] in 2015 to look into records and practices, including mortality rates, in Tuam and 13 other homes around the State. At the time of writing, the Commission was due to present its final report in 2020. In December 2018, the government announced its decision to forensically excavate the Tuam site.

'We let you down'

The family-state-church alliance, combined with poverty, also ensured a constant supply of unpaid labour for the country's ten so-called Magdalene laundries, secure residential institutions with commercial laundries run by religious orders. An estimated 10,000 women and girls ended up in these catch-all institutions over a 50-year period, with a quarter of referrals made or facilitated by the State.

These institutions were accepted by the wider community for generations as a kind of halfway-house for wayward or destitute women. The perception was that the girls must have been sent there for a good reason. People considered the nuns to be trustworthy guides and custodians for these young women from difficult backgrounds. Besides, the girls had no means and were deemed lucky to get bed and board. We now know that there was a harsh and punitive regime behind the walls of the laundries and too many young women were ill-treated and deprived of their liberty without due process. Magdalene laundries have become a byword for cruelty and injustice against Irish women.

The long-awaited spotlight finally turned to the laundries in the 1990s, long after the model had become redundant for social and economic reasons. At this stage, only small numbers of elderly, institutionalised women lived in such places, effectively in care. One example was the laundry at High Park in Drumcondra, surrounded by substantial grounds and owned by the Sisters of Our Lady of Charity of Refuge. This was a prime location near Dublin city centre. By 1989, the nuns wanted to redevelop their own residential buildings on the site and they secured planning permission for hundreds of houses on part of the land which they sold to fund the project. The sisters subsequently began preparations to sell another portion of the land, this time 11.5

acres. A graveyard for the home's residents on this section of the land had been in use for a century up to 1986 so the nuns were faced with the problem of disposing of the bodies before that parcel could be sold and developed. It took some time to get an exhumation licence sorted for 133 bodies before the exhumation began in August 1993, according to the Justice for Magdalenes Research group (jfmresearch.com).[v] But the funeral directors soon discovered there were more bodies than the 133 listed on the licence and the nuns had to apply for an additional exhumation licence for 22 more bodies. This discrepancy did not become public knowledge until ten years later through research carried out by investigative journalist Mary Raftery. But the media reports about the exhumation and cremation of 133 bodies were disturbing enough and marked the beginning of a long process of campaigning and reporting which increased awareness of the issue.

After many women came forward to share their stories of exploitation, public opinion forced the State to respond. An inter-departmental committee was set up to establish the facts of State involvement in laundries. When the government received the committee's report, then Taoiseach Enda Kenny offered a State apology in the Dáil in 2013 and a compensation scheme for victims was set up. A group of women were guests of honour at a special reception held by President Michael D Higgins at the presidential residence in June 2018. Some 220 survivors enjoyed the sunshine in the gardens of Áras an Uachtaráin and heard the president give full recognition to the injustice they suffered.

'Ireland failed you. When you were vulnerable and in need of the support of Irish society and its institutions, its authorities did not cherish you, protect you, respect your dignity or meet your needs, and so many in the wider society colluded with all that through their silence.'[vi]

So how did the unfortunate victims end up behind the walls of the laundries? The 2013 McAleese report[vii] that looked into the issue named three routes. The first was the criminal justice system, usually following conviction for petty crimes, 'everything from failure to purchase a train ticket to larceny, vagrancy, assault'. The second was girls who were referred directly from industrial or reformatory school, or while they were still under supervision after leaving school, in some cases until they reached the age of majority (which was 21 years of age during the heyday of the laundries). The third category was women or girls transferred from other health or social services, such as former residents of Mother and Baby homes, psychiatric patients, former foster children, people with learning disabilities, orphans, homeless women and girls from abusive homes. Most spent less than a year living there but the fact of having been in a laundry carried a great stigma which drove many to emigrate afterwards. The report found that many girls, especially those transferred from children's homes, had no idea why they were locked up or how long they would have to stay in the 'harsh and physically demanding work environment'. Cut off from the outside world, there was no real protection from cruel or vindictive behaviour from the nuns who referred to residents as penitents.

Fighting back

Biological destiny is writ large for Irish women. We have been fighting a war over women's bodies in Ireland for my entire life with some of the most tragic cases happening right up to the present day. It is hard to tell if the stranglehold on female reproductive health was motivated by a patriarchal urge to contain women or by truly-held beliefs about sexual morality and the sanctity of life. Perhaps a convenient fusion of the two.

Irish feminism has a long and proud organised history going back to the suffragettes, early trade unionists, social workers and revolutionaries. The idealists who wrote the 1916 Proclamation used inclusive, egalitarian language, promising equal opportunities to all citizens. The first elections of the Free State in 1922 were based on universal suffrage. But within a few years of independence, it became clear that women were not going to enjoy equal treatment. The conservative statesmen of the 1920s and 1930s embraced the *Kinder, Küche, Kirche* (children, kitchen, church) model for women that was popular in much of Europe at the time.

This was the period when restrictive labour laws were introduced for women's work, when the sale and importation of contraception was first banned and when women were denied full participation in civic life, such as the right to sit on juries. Many limitations were not written in law but stemmed from the burdens of domestic and maternal life.

By the time the government got round to drafting the Constitution in 1937, the position was clear. Article 40.1, which dealt with personal rights, states: 'All citizens shall, as human persons, be held equal before the law.' But this was swiftly qualified in the next breath with the line: 'This shall not be held to mean that the State shall not in its enactments have due regard to differences of capacity, physical and moral, and of social function.' No prizes for guessing the gender of the default person who is equal before the law or which half of the population might differ from that default citizen in their capacity or social function.

There was more. Wrapped in benevolent language, in Article 41 which dealt with family, the founding fathers wrote: 'In particular, the State recognises that by her life within the home, woman gives to the State a support without which the common good cannot be achieved. The State shall, therefore, endeavour to ensure that mothers shall not be obliged by economic necessity to engage in labour to the neglect of their duties in the home.'

There is a kind of protection that can cut both ways. It is not only someone with a modern-day perspective who would object. Voices of dissent were raised at the time but to no avail.

In a letter to the *Irish Independent* published on May 5th 1937, veteran feminist Hannah Sheehy Skeffington complained that the proposed Constitution was based on 'a Fascist Model, in which women would be relegated to permanent inferiority, their avocations and choice of callings limited because of an implied invalidism as the weaker sex.'

The playing field began to get more even in the 1960s with a growing economy and, by the end of the decade, free secondary education. Momentum for women's rights was gathering globally. In response to a United Nations directive, the government set up the Commission for the Status of Women in 1970. The commission was to report on the status of women in Ireland and make recommendations 'on the steps necessary to ensure the participation of women on equal terms and conditions with men in the political, social, cultural and economic life of the country'.

The 1970s is crowded with organisations and achievements which advanced the position of women. Before the commission's work was completed, the IWLM seized the initiative in 1971 by issuing its manifesto calling for six changes – equal rights, equal pay and equal educational opportunities, justice for single mothers, the right to contraception and housing. Divorce and abortion were just too much of a taboo to mention. The Commission for the Status of Women came through with similar recommendations and there was a rush of progress in 1973 with the removal of the marriage bar, which had forced women in the civil service and some private sector jobs to resign on marriage, and with the introduction of State benefits for deserted wives and unmarried mothers. A lot of the legislative change in favour of women, such as equal treatment in the workplace, protection of pregnant and breastfeeding workers, and rights to maternity and parental leave, was driven by the European Union and its forerunners.[viii]

Some of the organisations founded in the 1970s include the Council for the Status of Women, Irish Women's Aid to support the victims of intimate partner violence, Cherish to support single parents (which led a long campaign to have the status of illegitimacy scrapped, a change that didn't happen until 1987) and the Rape Crisis Centre in 1978. Nothing was given. Everything had to be pushed for and it was women who were doing the pushing, as leading feminist activist Ailbhe Smyth told me in an interview in Dublin.

'Irish women have changed Ireland, there's no doubt about it. The huge levels of socio-sexual change here were pushed by women. Maybe people think that should go without saying but actually I think it's really important. The pressure over the years to shift gender relations has profoundly changed Ireland and of course it's always women who do the shifting in that situation. If I compare the Ireland I grew up in and Ireland now, you're talking about completely different countries.'

Most recently, Smyth was doing the pushing as co-director of the successful Together 4 Yes campaign to repeal the Eighth Amendment in 2018. So, what was the Eighth Amendment to the Irish Constitution and where did it come from? It is evident that the controversial anti-abortion amendment was a direct consequence of the liberal reforms of the 1970s. All those social changes produced a backlash among conservatives who feared that abortion and divorce would be next. Abortion was already illegal in Ireland under harsh 19th-century legislation but there was a fear among certain circles that the courts might eventually open the door to legalising abortion as they had to contraception. A group of 13 Catholic organisations set up the Pro-Life Amendment Campaign in 1981, which ultimately got the backing of the people to change the Constitution in a 1983 referendum.

The Eighth Amendment of 1983 acknowledged the right to life of 'the unborn' without any definition. It said that the State guarantees in its laws to respect, defend and vindicate that right, with 'due regard to the equal right to life of the mother'.

The amendment was a pre-emptive strike and a highly effective one, too. This wording did not just mean that no regular abortion services could be made available in Ireland (until after repeal in 2018 as it turned out), it also enforced callous and dangerous restrictions in prenatal and maternity care. The complicated realities of unwanted pregnancy, pregnancy loss, fatal foetal abnormality, pregnancy by rape, pregnancy with serious illness, child pregnancy – all of it disregarded in one stroke. Hard cases, most infamously the Ms X case in 1992, a 14-year-old rape victim, kept coming up, challenging the unworkable rigidity of the Eighth Amendment. Other cases involved life-saving cancer treatment being withdrawn from pregnant women. The response was to insert more constitutional amendments, including the right to travel for abortion, and eventually to enact legislation in 2013 which defined the circumstances and processes within which abortion could be legally conducted.

The legislation followed a wave of national and international outrage in 2012 after it become known that a 31-year-old woman, Savita Halappanawar, had died of sepsis in a Galway hospital because she was denied a termination. Over 3 days, doctors refused to intervene to terminate Savita's 17-week-pregnancy as she and her husband requested, because of the legal position. This, even though she was enduring a long drawn-out miscarriage and there was no chance of the foetus surviving. By the time the miscarriage completed naturally, Halappanawar's health had deteriorated so much that she could not be saved.

But even the 2013 legislation did not change the material position of women in Savita Halappanawar's circumstances because of the wording of the constitution. A pregnant woman or girl with a physical illness or experiencing a medical emergency could only have a termination if there was a 'real and substantial risk' to her life if she did not have a termination. The same applied to suicidal women and children.

Suffering was fine. The woman or child could suffer any degree of physical or mental anguish but as long as her life was not in imminent danger, it didn't count. The woman's health or wellbeing during or after pregnancy did not matter. The unborn's right to life trumped her right to safety and peace of mind from day one.

Before the amendment was repealed by 66 per cent of voters in May 2018, Irish society had to endure news of more dreadful cases. In 2014, a rape victim and asylum seeker, Ms Y, was denied an abortion, even though she said she was suicidal as soon as she discovered the pregnancy. No State agency was willing or able to help her and the weeks ticked by. Because she had no travel documents, she was denied entry to the UK for the abortion she wanted and sent back to Ireland. By the time two psychiatrists assessed her and officially deemed her to be suicidal, it was too late – the pregnancy was viable. Ms Y went on hunger strike and had to be forcibly hydrated by court order. The baby was delivered by caesarean section at 25 weeks gestation.

There was worse to come. Christmas of 2014 was overshadowed by the case of a clinically-dead woman who was being kept on life support against her family's wishes because she was pregnant. The pregnancy was at 15 weeks gestation when the woman was declared dead from a massive brain trauma on December 3rd. Because of the equal right to life of the unborn, the doctors were thrown into a legal conundrum, which ended up in the High Court with lawyers acting for the hospital, the woman, her father and the unborn. The judgement came on December 26th, by which stage the woman's body was showing signs of decomposition.

'To maintain and continue the present somatic support for the mother would deprive her of her dignity in death and subject her father, her partner and her young children to unimaginable distress in a futile exercise which commenced only because of fears held by treating medical specialists of potential legal consequences,' the court said.

A formula of words in the Constitution reached in and distorted the relationship between doctors and their patients, as well as preventing Irish women from getting good quality aftercare on their return as criminals to Ireland. That this inhumane law stayed in place for so long is testament to a deep-rooted tradition in Ireland of silencing and shaming women, a tradition that had always been dependent on indifference to female suffering. And a tradition that was shaped and upheld by the Catholic Church.

The silencing finally came to an end during the Repeal the 8th campaign when women who had experienced abortion in ordinary and extraordinary circumstances started talking about the suffering the abortion ban had caused them. In a storytelling culture, the Repeal vote was won on first-hand testimonies of the cruelty of the law. It was as if voters were given the chance to make amends. As Ailbhe Smyth puts it:

'How horrible Ireland was to so many women for such a long time. And that's something we felt ashamed of and guilty about as well. And while those kinds of words were never used on the surface in the campaign, I think that feeling was really there. The realisation that we could not hold our heads up in good conscience as a people unless we said, we've got to do right by women now.'

Leading from the front

For most of the history of the State, women only had a cameo role in Irish politics. Women TDs tended to be daughters of well-established politicians who were elected on the strength of their deceased father's reputation. That is not to say that there were no examples of women who made their own mark, with or without connections. Former European Commissioner, Máire Geoghegan-Quinn, the first woman to hold a cabinet post since Constance Markievicz in 1922, went on to have a solid career. One of her personal highlights was the role she played as minister for justice in 1993 in decriminalising homosexuality. Mary O'Rourke, once known as the Mammy of the Dáil, was another formidable Fianna Fáil politician who followed in her father's footsteps but forged a strong reputation of her own. Meanwhile Mary Harney, the youngest ever member of the Seanad at 24, was the first female Tánaiste and the first to lead a political party when she became head of the Progressive Democrats in 1993.

Since then, every party has attracted strong female leaders, notably former Tánaistí Joan Burton of Labour and Frances Fitzgerald of Fine Gael, as well as Mary Lou McDonald, the leader of Sinn Féin. Not to mention that two of the last three presidents have been called Mary – Mary Robinson and Mary McAleese.

Impressive. Does this mean that Irish women are adequately

Máire Geoghegan-Quinn became a cabinet Minister in 1979, the first woman to do so since Constance Markievicz in 1922.

represented in politics? Not by a long shot. But at least the problem is not being left alone to fix itself any more. The Electoral (Amendment) (Political Funding) Act 2012 introduced gender quotas for national politics, requiring political parties to select at least 30 per cent of candidates of each gender for national elections or else lose 50 per cent of their State funding for the parliamentary term. Amazing what effect a little financial pressure can have. The next election in 2016 saw an increase in the number of female candidates running and elected. The breakdown in the Dáil rose to 35 women out of 158, an increase from 15 to 22 per cent.

Writing in *The Irish Times* supplement marking 100 years since Irish women won the vote in 1918, Senator Ivana Bacik named the five Cs which are barriers to women's representation in politics: childcare, cash, confidence, culture and candidate selection procedures. She welcomed the progress made in the

2016 election, which moved Ireland up to the middle of the field of OECD countries in terms of representation, but said the figure was still far too low.

'We are continuing to work to increase the numbers of women entering politics through initiatives like the very welcome establishment of the Oireachtas Women's Caucus last year.' The caucus is seeking the extension of quotas to local elections which is where many politicians cut their teeth before going on to be elected at national level. Currently just 22 per cent of councillors are women, a result described by the Women's Council of Ireland as 'very disappointing'.

Over the past decade or more, much ink has been spilt about the representation of women in various areas of Irish life. We have had a National Women's Strategy for 2006 - 2017, followed by a National Strategy for Women and Girls 2017-2020. Its goal is 'an Ireland where all women enjoy equality with men and can achieve their full potential, while enjoying a safe and fulfilling life'.

The current strategy tells us that the number of female judges has tripled in the past two decades. One third of judges and four of the nine members of the Supreme Court are now women.

A target was set in 1992 that women should make up 40 per cent of State boards. The target has been met by half of the total, which is now chasing an enhanced target of 45 per cent. Similar moves are under way in the civil service which have produced relatively quick results.

These radical ideas seem to be catching. In November 2018, another Mary, Minister for Higher Education Mary Mitchell O'Connor, announced plans to fund 45 female-only professorships over three years to tackle gender inequality in academia. In the university sector half of all lecturers are women but only one in four professors are women. The minister's taskforce for gender equality[ix] found that it would take another 20 years to achieve gender balance at professor level if things were left to develop naturally. So she decided, to hell with that.

'I believe that gender inequality exists because of systemic and cultural barriers that have solidified over time. We must work together to tear down these barriers,' Mitchell O'Connor said.

If policymakers are looking for ideas on how best to tear down barriers, inspiration is close at hand. In *The Economist's* Glass Ceiling Index of the best and worst countries to be a working woman, five of the top six slots were occupied by Nordic countries in 2018. Ireland ranks 21st out of 29 countries.[x]

So much for the public and higher education sectors, what about private companies? The infamous leaky pipeline is just as leaky in Ireland. Women continue to be fairly represented at the lowest management level but lose ground in middle management and drop away significantly at senior executive and board level. But there is definitely movement here. Between 2007 and 2016, the proportion of female non-executive directors of corporate boards more than doubled to 16 per cent.

All of this momentum suggests that it is a good time to be a mid-career, ambitious woman in Ireland. But not everyone has that privilege. A lot of women have jobs rather than careers, often part-time jobs. Almost 70 per cent of all part-time workers are women. A 2017 ESRI study[xi] found that women were more than twice as likely to be earning the minimum wage (6.9 % of women employees versus 2.7% of male employees). According to the study this difference is largely related to an increased likelihood of working part-time and a higher concentration of women in lower-paid sectors such as retail, accommodation and food. Do these women jump or are they pushed? The study said that further research is required to understand to what extent choice comes into this uneven outcome.

I am not sure if this question can be answered satisfactorily because so much comes down to individual relationships and situations, as illustrated beautifully by Dominique Cleary in her essay about motherhood (see end of chapter). Women working and raising children largely on their own face particular challenges. Nine out of ten one-parent households are headed by women. In a country with the most expensive childcare in the world, the barriers facing these mothers are the highest. But there are barriers within relationships too. Women in two-parent households may not be in a position to negotiate equal partnership when it comes to combining working hours with childcare and domestic duties. Traditional roles do not fade away overnight, and maternity leave sets a precedent for mothers to be the lead parent indefinitely. Many employers have adapted slowly and reluctantly to family-friendly practices, mainly geared towards their female employees. It hardly suits them to do the same for fathers too. So, when the majority of fathers do not avail of the unpaid parental leave to which they are entitled, how much choice comes into that uneven outcome? There is more leaning in to be done by fathers, mothers and employers, or at least leaning towards each other. The new means-based State subsidy for childcare, rolled out in 2019, should help somewhat.

Meanwhile, the gender pay gap has been gradually narrowing and is now below the EU average at 13.9 per cent according to the latest Eurostat figures which are from 2014. Legislation introducing compulsory gender pay gap reporting by employers is in the pipeline. Unfortunately 40 years of equal pay legislation did not get the job done.

Because people tend to be secretive about their salaries, it is rare to find a good example of the gender pay gap but RTÉ news anchor Sharon Ní Bheoláin did us all a favour in 2017 when she spoke out about the difference in salary between her and her co-host Brian Dobson on the evening news programme, *Six-One*. The difference in annual salary was in the range of €60,000 to €80,000.

Both Ní Bheoláin and Dobson responded to the scandal with refreshing frankness. In an interview the following year on RTÉ's *Late Late Show*[xii], Dobson spoke of the turning point currently faced by society with regard to the role of women.

'I say this as a man. I think it's a thoroughly good, healthy development because I think men are actually in some ways disadvantaged by this very patriarchal society that we're expected to carry. I don't think it'll do men any harm, actually, if there's a bit of a shift towards greater respect for women, greater equality for women, greater involvement for women in decision-making in every aspect of society.'

Contemporary Irish society is rightly proud of all the extraordinary women who have achieved every imaginable success, from winning international literary prizes to gold medals in boxing to Irish farmer of the year. We will continue to see successes in the arts, the economy, sports and public life, and the country will benefit from that excellence. But we can't all live our lives on that level. My family is full of inspiring women who achieved things on a more ordinary scale. I grew up in a three-generation household where both my mother and grandmother worked as teachers. When my mother retired, she became a full-time carer, looking after my disabled father at home for the last years of his life. We sisters have always helped look after each other's children as much as we could to square the circle of combining work and family life.

It took me the longest time to work out the best title for this chapter. When I look at all the challenges that have been overcome in my lifetime, it seems to me as if Irish women have been on a difficult journey through rough seas and are only now reaching safe harbour. Where will that energy go now? Somewhere good, I feel. To go back to the three nominees for the archetypal Irishwoman, the fairest result is for the award to be shared by all three. Our Irishwoman has known suffering but it no longer defines her. She discovered her inner warrior queen and fought her way to her rightful place, whether that's in the highest office in the land or as an honoured guest at the President's garden party. Her enduring joy is the loyalty and love of everyone she's ever cared for. She is a force to be reckoned with.

In Focus: Dominique Cleary

This is an excerpt from an essay by Dominique Cleary called 'Advice on Motherhood', first published in The Dublin Review *in its Autumn 2018 issue. In the essay Cleary lists all the people who had some comment to make on her role as a mother, from her Ecuadorian grandmother to her boss to Doris Lessing. This passage entitled 'The Security guard at work' is a little slice of life that shows some of the pressure faced by new mothers. It takes place at the end of Cleary's workday in a Dublin office.*

'At some point I began to notice that the phone on my desk had a tendency to ring just as I was getting up to leave at 5.30. I often ignored the phone and sneaked through the shadows in the corridors that led to my locked bicycle in the car park. I recited a mantra in my head to dispel the guilt: *Nothing here is a matter of life or death. Everything can wait until tomorrow.* I justified myself to myself by counting the hours since I had left Robyn in the morning: nine wakeful hours, motherless.

One day, when I thought I had made a clean escape, I was stopped by the security guard at the gates of the car park. Someone had transferred a call for me down to his kiosk, and I wondered if it had been done out of spite. The security guard was holding the receiver out the window at me. He told me I had better take it. I considered making a final burst for freedom, but we had locked eyes, and it seemed impossible. I took notes on a pad resting on the handlebars. It wasn't an important or a particularly long call, maybe just under ten minutes, but it was enough to set off my panic about arriving late at the crèche. I tried to get some momentum into my pedalling but I was breathless with choked-up fury and frustration. It was hard to cycle and cry at the same time.'[xiii]

Endnotes
_____

[i] https://cso.ie/en/media/csoie/releasespublications/documents/birthsdm/archivedreports/P-VS_1971.pdf

[ii] Chains or Change, a manifesto published by the Irish Women's Liberation Movement 1971

[iii] http://www.adoptionloss.ie/history.htm

[iv] http://www.mbhcoi.ie/mbh.nsf/page/Terms%20of%20reference-en

[v] http://jfmresearch.com/home/preserving-magdalene-history/high-park/

[vi] https://www.irishexaminer.com/breakingnews/ireland/ireland-failed-you-president-higgins-apologises-to-magdalene-laundries-survivors-at-aras-an-uachtarain-event-846951.html

[vii] http://www.justice.ie/en/JELR/Pages/MagdalenRpt2013

[viii] https://ec.europa.eu/ireland/node/684_en

[ix] https://hea.ie/assets/uploads/2018/11/Gender-Equality-Taskforce-Action-Plan-2018-2020.pdf

[x] https://www.economist.com/graphic-detail/2018/02/15/the-glass-ceiling-index

[xi] https://www.esri.ie/system/files/media/file-uploads/2017-10/BKMNEXT332.pdf

[xii] 30.03.2018

[xiii] 'Advice on Motherhood' by Dominique Cleary, first published in *The Dublin Review*, Autumn 2018

CHAPTER 8

The Irish Economy is a Poster Child

The Irish economy has been busy in recent years, impressing and baffling observers in equal measure. It was the poster child for phenomenal growth during the Celtic Tiger boom of 1994–2008, followed by the poster child for austerity from 2008. The economy is currently double-jobbing as the poster child for recovery and globalisation. I'm talking about the new Irish economy which only came into being through mysterious alchemy around 1995. This is a totally different creature from the old Irish economy over which it is tempting to draw a veil.

Yet if you want to understand the boom-bust see-saw of the last three decades you need to go back to the 1980s, the low point of Irish independence and economic progress. That decade provides the key to what went before and what came afterwards, especially Irish spending fever. The soundtrack of the 1980s for me was the ping-ping of raindrops falling into saucepans inside our house.

One economic indicator says it all – job creation. The Central Statistics Office (CSO) recorded job growth of 3.1 per cent, or 66,800 additional people at work, in 2017, and 50,500 new jobs (2.3 per cent) in 2018. Taken together, that tops the number of jobs created in the first 60 years of the Irish state (100,000), which brought us up to 1982. In a nutshell: the economy can now generate more jobs in two years than it was formerly able to generate in six decades. The past truly is another country.

Before we turn back the clock, here is a snapshot of the shiny, happy Irish economy of today. Consistently scoring the highest growth rate in the European Union, it is an economy of superlatives, with unemployment down around 5 per cent, an improvement of 10 percentage points since 2012. With a workforce of 2.3 million, there are more people employed now than at the height of the boom in 2007 (though the population has grown by almost half a million). Disposable incomes are rising for all groups, and the mean annual household disposable income (net income after tax and social deductions) in 2017 was a not-too-shabby €48,476, according to the CSO survey on income and living conditions. Exports in 2018 reached €140 billion, the highest annual total on record. Shiny and happy – ish. There is some botox involved, amongst other things. The global supply of Allergan Pharmaceuticals' star drug is manufactured in Westport, County Mayo, one of many pharma bestsellers made in Ireland. Pfizer produces most of the global supply of Viagra in Ringaskiddy, County Cork. One third of Irish exports is made up of medical and pharmaceutical products alone, the vast majority produced by multinationals. Meanwhile, levels of consistent poverty (6.7 per cent) and enforced deprivation (18.8 per cent) are still relatively high but falling.

Allergan, Westport, County Mayo

What's another year?

Returning to that blighted decade that fashion and compassion forgot. There were five general elections in the 1980s, a referendum to introduce divorce that was rejected and a referendum giving us an amendment to the constitution effectively banning abortion in any circumstances for the next 35 years that was passed. If good things happened in the 1980s, I cannot recall them. Ann Lovett, the tragic 15-year-old schoolgirl from Granard, County Longford, was the most famous girl of my generation. Feeling unable to turn to anyone for help with her pregnancy, she died along with her baby after giving birth alone outdoors at the village grotto in January 1984.

In the North we began the decade with the hunger strikes, adding to the constant drip-drip of death and destruction across the border. Net emigration for the decade in the Republic of Ireland was over 200,000[i] and almost one third of the population was living under the poverty line. The population was a full 1.2 million smaller than today, at a mere 3.5 million. The weekly dole payment for a single person in 1985 was around £35 and the unemployment rate climbed to an all-time high of 17.3 per cent in December of that year. Amid restricted access to contraception, Ireland was a place of big families and little room. Six of my mother's eight siblings lived outside the country. When I say the only bright spot was Johnny Logan's white suit in the Eurovision Song Contest, I am not joking.

Meanwhile our crooked leader on and off for those years, Charlie Haughey of Fianna Fáil, who preached to the nation that we were living beyond our means[ii], lived a wildly extravagant lifestyle on bribes, stolen funds and overdrafts. His Taoiseach's salary of £51,036 a year could not have sustained even two months of a lifestyle that included, as Justine McCarthy detailed in a 1999 article[iii] in the *Irish Independent* when the Moriarty Tribunal was investigating Haughey's finances:

'... fine art and objets d'art, a mansion home, his own island, a farm, two holiday homes, a yacht, racehorses, helicopter commuting, vintage wines, a large household staff, a female companion, frequent dinners in the private room of one of Dublin's most expensive restaurants, and a bespoke Parisian wardrobe.'

The seventies had seen some bumpy progress but the second oil crisis in 1979 did not augur well for the upcoming decade and sealed Ireland's diagnosis as the sick man of Europe. The boom years of 1977 and 1978 had prompted a government spending spree that ended up leaving the country in a vulnerable position. The clawback, when it came a few years later, was painful, especially in punitive tax increases for Pay As You Earn (PAYE) workers.

According to the CSO, real average earnings fell by 4.5 per cent between 1980 and 1992, mainly due to high inflation. And did I mention debt? The debt to GDP ratio reached 150 per cent in the 1980s.

Now it all makes sense. I thought I had imagined the feelings of insecurity but no, my childhood really did take place against the backdrop of continuous crisis: the 1979-1992 macroeconomic crisis. In our house, the economic gloom manifested itself in that leaking roof and a dread of utility bills. Summer holidays were spent staying with relatives, the car was always parked pointing outwards to the main road in case a push-start was needed. And we were the privileged ones, with the teacher's salary my mother was bringing in plus my father's more sporadic commission cheques from selling toys and stationary for an English company.

Meanwhile, all was not well with the national currency, which had an impact on shopkeepers' willingness to buy from my father's catalogue. Tied to sterling on a one-to-one currency peg since its creation in 1927, the Irish pound or punt only split from the mother currency when Ireland joined the European Monetary System (EMS) in March 1979 and the British stayed out. A decade of fluctuation followed with the British to Irish exchange rate hopping between a high (for the Irish) of 1.03 and a low of 1.34 to reach 1.20 by 1989.

After all that, if any good news came along, by God we were going to celebrate it, and if any money come along, by God we were going to spend it. The 1980s were a dam behind which a lot of potential energy built up, both economic and societal.

EMS membership for the Irish pound (1979) eventually paid off, delivering low inflation by the mid-eighties and bringing interest rates down. Economic growth was beginning to recover by the late 1980s, which was a favourable climate for the initial discussions on European Monetary Union taking place in Europe. Ireland went on to vote, by almost 70 per cent, to accept the Maastricht Treaty in 1992 which created the Single Market. The euro was not far behind, becoming Ireland's currency in 1999.

Kiss me, I'm Irish

A cluster of feel-good events in the 1990s have been pointed to as potential catalysts for the Celtic Tiger that was waiting to spring in 1993 / 1994. They all took place in the context of a younger, well-educated population in comparison to other Western economies. The Irish soccer team made it to the quarter finals of the 1990 World Cup in Italy unleashing unprecedented scenes of joy and celebration. That same year, Mary Robinson, a lawyer and senator who had built a career campaigning for social justice and women's rights was elected Ireland's first woman president. In 1991 the Irish Pub Company formed, bringing a new packaged form of Irishness to foreign cities. It went on to install more than 1,800 Irish-themed watering holes in more than 50 countries over the next 15 years.[iv] My generation not only had the newfound opportunity to be employed in every major city in the world pulling pints but we experienced the novel sensation of associating our nation with success, with achievements of which we could be proud.

With three consecutive wins in the Eurovision Song Contest, in 1992, 1993 and 1994, Ireland was suddenly the darling of Europe but the real *pièce de resurgence* was yet to come. Irish dancing was about to be transformed from an old-fashioned hobby to a sexy new profession, thanks to *Riverdance*. The sensational interval act of the 1994 Eurovision in Dublin was developed into a hit show familiar to 25 million people who have seen it performed live all over the world.

This new pride in Irish culture was real, with all-Irish schools springing up like mushrooms. But it was also quick to be packaged and co-opted into selling Ireland as a tourist destination as well as a place to locate companies. In addition to having more job opportunities, there was a beneficial change of atmosphere of self-confidence for those of us making a living in Ireland. We had turned a corner. In May 1997, the map of Ireland glowed on the front page of *The Economist* under the caption, 'Europe's shining light'.

A time for peace

Even the Northern Ireland conflict obliged, with an IRA ceasefire in 1994 and tangible progress towards a lasting settlement which finally came in the form of the Good Friday Agreement in 1998. The peace dividend is often underestimated in the analysis of the skyrocketing economic growth of that era. Not only did it remove a major negative association of Ireland with violence that had long

Riverdance has now been seen by 25 million people around the world.

been a handicap, it also freed the government to shift its main focus from security to economic matters. On a psychological level, a better deal for the nationalist population in the North gave us in the guilty South permission to be happy.

Meanwhile, the law was finally catching up with social realities and a new language of tolerance became mainstream, as seen in the decriminalisation of homosexuality in 1993 and the acceptance of divorce by referendum in 1995. The ties of shame and censure that had bound the population were finally loosening. For once Ireland was not caught in a perfect storm but a perfect rainbow.

The economic success stories in these years were staggering. The country turned into one big building site with new streets, new city quarters, new restaurants, shopping centres, hotels and housing estates springing up at a relentless pace. By 2007, one in nine workers was employed in construction.

Incredibly, there was a 67 per cent increase in the total numbers in employment in Ireland between 1988 and 2004. Almost three-quarters of a million new jobs were created.[v] Unemployment reached a low of 3.6 per cent in 2001 while real GDP was increasing by 10 per cent per year[vi]. In 1996, Ireland became a country of sustained net immigration for the first time.

All this momentum was underpinned by social partnership, established in 1987, another trump in Ireland's hand. A series of successive deals between the social partners – government, the main employer groups and unions – were agreed to every three years, with unions accepting moderate wage increases in return for low income tax rates.

A time to spend

When things started improving for Ireland in the 1990s, a taut elastic was released. The result was a spectacular rise to prosperity that lasted until 2008, which earned Ireland the moniker 'Celtic Tiger.' This juggernaut of success was brought to a screeching halt by an economic crash, again phenomenal in scale but relatively brief, before a strong recovery, again phenomenal, took hold. Now that the recovery is breaking records, it is tempting to see the crash as the blip that interrupted our more natural state of 'boominess'. But only if you have a very short memory.

Ireland's overnight success from the late 1990s on did not escape international notice with 'econo-tourists' from around the world coming to witness and research the phenomenon first hand. International editorial writers raved about the country's dizzying rise to prosperity. By the time *The Economist* rated Ireland as having 'the highest economic quality of life in the world' in 2005, the hubris of Irish political and business leaders had reached its peak.

In July 2007, the Taoiseach Bertie Ahern made the now infamous remark, for which he later apologised, about a favourite target of his: begrudgers, or people who talked down the economy. 'Sitting on the sidelines, cribbing and moaning is a lost opportunity. I don't know how people who engage in that don't commit suicide because frankly the only thing that motivates me is being able to actively change something.[vii]' But the moaners were soon to be proved right.

From 1992 on, the Single Market made it easy to move goods and services within the EU. That came on top of years of generous EU funding for agriculture and infrastructure. For US companies that wanted to access the EU market, Ireland was a highly attractive English-speaking, business-friendly base. Bargain basement corporate tax rates were a major carrot too. The corporate tax rate in Ireland is still 12.5 per cent, compared to 19% in the UK, 24% in Italy, 25% in the Netherlands and Spain, 30% in Germany, 33.3 % in France and 21% in the US.

The US computer chip giant Intel led the way when it decided to locate its European manufacturing operations in Leixlip, Co Kildare in 1989, lured by IDA grants that totalled £87 million (€110 million). Many more firms followed so that job creation from foreign direct investment became a standing item on the news with ministers hopping from county to county cutting ribbons for the cameras.

But Irish consumers' willingness to spend money played a big part in the boom too. After so many years of cutting corners, we had some serious catching up to do. Irish shoppers filled their trollies with the finer things in life, masterfully and wickedly captured by Anne Enright in her description of Constance's supermarket shopping on Christmas Eve in *The Green Road*. There was a travel boom (Irish people on skis!), a home improvement boom, a car sales boom and an alcohol consumption boom, but most significantly for the Irish economy there was a housing boom.

There was no escaping the property mania of the late 1990s and 2000s. Prices were rising so fast that everyone wanted to get in on the game. After a while the prices moved so far above any kind of intrinsic value that normal rules no longer applied. Ireland was abuzz with conversations about crazy prices paid for houses, and stories about the profits people were making who had bought five years before, two years, one year. People were buying houses with siblings, with friends, building houses in their parents' gardens, moving 100 kilometres away, anything to get a foot on the ladder. Without a deposit, I saw no way into the magic circle of homeowners and so I opted out of that particular race. Eventually, I was so sick of the word property, I was glad to emigrate in the hope that I would never have to talk about it again.

But for old times' sake, I will talk property prices again, because property is firmly back on the agenda, raising the national blood pressure again. The average house price nationally in 1995 was £61,527 (€78,123). Prices increased steadily at a rate of double digits for the next 12 years, reaching a peak of €345,000 for an average property by 2007. When property prices fell off the cliff soon afterwards, they kept going down until, by 2013, prices had halved from the peak level. Prices are back up again now, with a national average asking price of €254,000 in 2018. We are still below the peak but the upward pressure is back with a vengeance, made worse by a chronic shortage of social housing. There is even more pressure on the rental sector where prices in 2018 had soared 30 per cent above their 2008 peak, according to daft.ie. The rapid expansion of unregulated short-term letting through websites like Airbnb exacerbated the problem as landlords switched potential homes to tourist accommodation, in some cases evicting tenants to do so. By 2018, there were two to three times as many Dublin properties available on Airbnb as were listed for regular long-term rental. It remains to be seen whether a newly-imposed limit on the number of days per year landlords can rent out second properties will have the effect of freeing up more properties for regular renters.

The current housing crisis is causing stress and suffering on a significant scale. It is the topic of the moment. If you look at the small ads boards at supermarkets, you will see neatly written cards pinned up by people who have been approved for the local authorities' housing assistance payment. Forlornly, they beg for potential landlords to take them on. A one-bedroom apartment in Tallaght, Dublin, listed online in January 2019 had more than 4,000 views in the first 24 hours. RTÉ ran the second season of *This Crowded House*, a documentary series which follows the stories of young people trying to move out of home – an impossible challenge for some. It is difficult for single people of any age on modest incomes. At my school reunion, an old friend who lives in her mother's house said she was considering buying a prefab – 'residential log cabin' – to put in the garden just to get her own space. In the summer of 2018, I viewed a so-called studio with another friend, a converted garage with a price tag of over €900 per month attached to a nice family home. You would need to keep the blinds drawn permanently for any privacy. My friend was almost desperate enough to take the shoebox but she drew the line when the landlady said no overnight guests were allowed. No sex please, we're Irish landlords.

A nation of speculators

What caused the property bubble that burst in 2008? Let's see what the experts say. In the analysis of *The Economy of Ireland, Policy-Making in a Global Context (2017)*, edited by John O'Hagan and Francis O'Toole, there were five main reasons: the new euro currency which delivered cheap credit, households that were comfortable (you could say very comfortable) with borrowing, the expansion of tax incentives by the government, inexperienced Irish regulators who suffered from the 'this time it's different' trap that accompanies every crash, and cheap Eastern European labour bringing the costs down.

In his seminal work on the demise of the Celtic Tiger, *Ship of Fools*, Fintan O'Toole is more accusatory in his analysis of who was to blame. The core problem was land, or how land supply was being handled. Ireland has no shortage of land but it has a shortage of transparency around land ownership and transactions. For years, landowners and property speculators were making fortunes behind the scenes from zoning decisions. Money also changed hands with crooked politicians involved in those decisions. Then, speculators were being permitted to sit on vast tracts of land around Dublin, ramping up demand and eventually house prices. O'Toole pulls no punches. Part of the problem was, he writes, that Fianna Fail was very close to the people who gained most from high property prices – the builders and developers.

'Another part, however, was the self-generating nature of a demand for expensive houses. Ireland gradually became a nation of speculators, betting on endless rises in house prices. People who already had houses at the start of the boom had an interest in seeing their values rise. People who bought houses at inflated prices had the same interest. The more people who were suckered into borrowing beyond their means to acquire houses for up to twice their real worth, the larger the critical mass of voters for whom the idea of the government acting to make houses cheaper was anathema.'[viii] To back up this claim, O'Toole reminds us that Irish banks approved 1.1 million mortgages for house purchases between 1995 and 2008.

Meanwhile, storm clouds were gathering for the global economy and Ireland was on track to take the hardest hit. In March 2008, award-winning Anglo Irish Bank, darling of the banking sector, announced that it was taking a write-down on risky assets and adopting a more cautious approach to lending. The news came as a bombshell since Anglo had been lauded as Europe's most successful bank. Behind the scenes, its commercial lending bubble had burst. The Anglo business model depended on a constantly expanding property market. It had been lending money to the country's biggest developers for ever more extravagant schemes and was crazily over-exposed to one sector. As part of the fallout of the US property crash, banks were unable to borrow money on the international market, which brought the flawed Anglo business model to a shuddering halt. There was nothing to stop the Anglo loan book from imploding, along with Anglo's share price, which had fallen to worthless by Christmas 2008.

As far back as 2000, a former Central Bank regulator, William Slattery, had warned about the danger of unsustainable lending leading to negative equity of as much as 30 to 50 per cent. This is exactly what happened in 2008 to the later crop of property buyers, who had paid inflated prices because they had felt under such pressure to get their foot on the damn ladder.

The debt burden was twofold – public and private: In the five years to 2007, Irish households had piled up mortgage, overdraft and credit card debt, doubling the amount they owed to more than two years' income per household on average.

Guaranteed disaster

But the real squeeze was on a national level. Without new money to lend, the pyramid collapsed and the banks were left with bad debts of some €85 billion. September 29, 2008 was a disastrous day on the Irish stock exchange with bank stocks in freefall and rumours that the banks would not be able to open for business the next day. The financial institutions were at the heart of the economy. As RTÉ's David Murphy put it. 'If they failed, the patient died.' That night, faced with the prospect of a run on potentially insolvent Irish banks, the government took the drastic decision to extend a State guarantee to the six main Irish banks for two years. The guarantee covered the banks' deposits, loans and obligations. In practice this amounted to €375 billion or twice the country's GDP. Ireland was not the only country to extend a bank guarantee in 2008 but its guarantee was the highest in relation to GDP and it included bondholders.

In a 2015 evaluation report looking back on Ireland's bailout, the European Commission explained the link that was established between bank debt and national debt due to the bank guarantee: '... the solvency of the Irish sovereign [system] and that of the banking system became directly intertwined. This eventually turned the banking crisis into a sovereign debt crisis...'[ix]

The guarantee wasn't enough. The three largest banks – Bank of Ireland, AIB and Anglo – needed to be recapitalised, and the government, under the leadership of finance minister Brian Lenihan, prepared to do just that in early 2009.

Anglo was in the worst shape by far, and irregularities came to light involving hidden loans to its top executives. When it became clear that recapitalisation would not save the bank, the government nationalised Anglo in January 2009. But the deception at Anglo went deeper than anyone could have imagined. Starbucks now occupies Anglo's former headquarters on St. Stephen's Green. Customers can enjoy a sugar rush in the same place that bankers once hatched the scheme that nearly bankrupted the country. The bank's top managers used a

The government nationalised Anglo Irish Bank in January 2009 having discovered the serious irregularities involving hidden loans to its top executives.

fraudulent circular accounting scheme, moving money in and out of another bank so that it looked like new money coming in. This was done to paper over the giant hole in the centre of the bank's finances and the fraud ultimately cheated the Irish tax payer to the tune of billions.

In February 2009, the government moved ahead with the bailout of Bank of Ireland and AIB, providing initial loans of €3.5 billion each in exchange for shares. Both banks eventually needed more money but they managed to avert total disaster. Bank of Ireland paid back its loans in full by 2014 and AIB is still working on it. A decade later the State still owns some 70 per cent of AIB and 14 per cent of Bank of Ireland.

On top of these banking woes, tax revenue had already collapsed so the government was forced to borrow to pay for social welfare and the day-to-day running of the country. In what seemed like the blink of an eye, Ireland was transformed from international success story to economic basketcase.

S.O.S.

Say the words bailout, troika or bondholders to an Irish person and you will see them work up a lather of outrage. When the two-year bank guarantee was up in 2010, the Irish government saw itself facing a 'funding cliff' with a wave of debt in the form of bonds maturing in September. It had fully included bonds in the guarantee, unlike other countries' guarantees which only pledged to cover a percentage.

The public finances were in dire straits and the climax was reached in what was perceived by many citizens as the humiliation of Ireland. In November 2010, after a build-up of pressure from the European Central Bank (ECB), which was by then shouldering the cost of the Irish bank guarantee, the government formally applied to enter 'a programme' with the European Commission, the ECB and the IMF, otherwise known as the Troika[x]. This was a bailout package that amounted to €67.5 billion (around 40 per cent of GDP that year). In return for financial aid Ireland would get its act together and implement the agreed programme. Efforts by the Irish government to get the Troika to agree to senior debt holders of the six Irish banks accepting some of the losses ('burning the bondholders') to recoup some of the cost of the bailout were blocked by the ECB.

To the relief of the Irish negotiators, the Troika accepted the Irish plea not to have its cheekily low corporate tax rate included in the negotiations. The Fianna Fáil-Green Party (plus Independents) government had prepared a national recovery plan for 2011-2014 which was then accepted by the Troika as a central plank of the negotiations, along with a range of measures to restructure the banking system and prune it to a healthier size to get it out of too-big-to-fail territory (assets five times GDP). The plan involved savings of €10 billion through spending cuts and €5 billion to be raised through higher taxes over the four-year period. The new Fine Gael-led government, which came into office in March 2011, negotiated some adjustments but stuck to the overall plan, gaining the Irish economy a new role as 'the poster child for austerity'.

By December 2013, when Ireland completed the bailout programme successfully and exited, the IMF was full of praise: 'Ireland has pulled back from an exceptionally deep banking crisis, significantly improved its fiscal position, and regained its access to the international financial markets'.[xi] However, the people were not impressed and a new hostile constituency of voters emerged who would never forgive the government for austerity, on which every national failing was blamed. This anger found a focus in the national movement against water charges which culminated in a payment boycott and huge protests in 2014-2015.

The public debt that was racked up in a pretty short space of time peaked at 123 per cent of GDP in 2013. It is now down to 64.8 per cent, at just over €200 billion, the EU target of 60 per cent of GDP finally within sight.

Comeback kid

Recessions caused by banking crises are notoriously long and recoveries muted, OECD economist David Haugh observed in 2016[xii]. Why has the expansion in Ireland been so strong? Foreign investment is Haugh's answer.

'Between 2009 and 2013, an extraordinary €125 billion (61% of GDP) of foreign direct investment (FDI) flowed into Ireland. Even in the midst of the banking and fiscal crisis and emigration surge, quietly, almost under the radar, foreign capital and brains continued to flow into Ireland.'

Spearheading this resurgence were the Silicon Docks on the quays of the River Liffey in Dublin, the location of Ireland's information technology cluster. Familiar global names such as Google, Facebook, Twitter and Airbnb have made nests in this new, trendy area, nests that are feathered with soft-touch tax arrangements. Meanwhile, 'eight of the top 10 global pharmaceutical companies have a significant presence in Ireland, centred on Cork, while half of the world's top 50 banks and top 20 insurance companies operate out of the International Financial Services Centre in Dublin,' David Haugh also observed.

On the election trail in 2011, the future Taoiseach Enda Kenny claimed he would make Ireland the best small country in the world to do business. When it comes to international rankings, Ireland does well. Ireland is the second most competitive economy in the EU with the highest level of growth of the 28 members in 2018 (8.2 per cent), and the seventh most competitive economy in the world.[xiii]

Some lessons have been learned from all the pain. By 2019, 1 in 16 workers were directly employed in construction, compared to 1 in 9 back in 2007. The banks are on a tighter leash due to better regulation and better oversight. Irish household debt, though still in the top five in Europe, is falling steadily. The Central Bank of Ireland has created a new measure for the economy called modified gross national income (GNI*), about 40 per cent smaller than GDP, to filter out the distortion caused by multinational tax schemes. But behind the new wave of high exports, fast growth and job creation lie some weaknesses in the Irish economy that cannot be ignored. Combined with Brexit, potentially an external shock extraordinaire, these weaknesses could be our undoing a second time.

Warning signs

A chorus of warning voices can be heard about Ireland having too many eggs in one basket but there are no quick solutions to changing the outcome of more than 50 years of policy. The Public Accounts Committee and the Irish Fiscal Advisory Council have issued warnings about over-reliance on corporation tax. With a slightly different slant, speaking on *Morning Ireland* on RTÉ Radio in July 2018, Professor Peter Clinch of the National Competitiveness Council sounded the alarm: 'Ireland is flying off one large engine. A very small number of companies exporting a very small number of goods and services to a very small number of markets.' The figures are striking: one third of Irish exports are accounted for by just 5 companies and 10 companies alone pay about 40 per cent of corporation tax.

But economist David McWilliams tells us[xiv] not to worry that foreign-owned multinationals accounted for 80 per cent of corporate tax receipts in 2017 and previous years. He pooh-poohs the notion that the tax take is fragile or likely to evaporate at the stroke of a corporate pen many miles away. Writing on his website in 2018, he argued that other countries don't worry about multinational corporations disappearing so the Irish should get over their fear of being dumped.

'The supposition is that simply because these firms are not headquartered in Ireland, using Irish-based capital (whatever that means), or don't have a board made up of Irish citizens, in some way their presence in the economy is illegitimate and built on sand.'

McWilliams' confidence is reassuring. I went to Trinity College to meet Professor John O'Hagan for some answers on the Irish economy. At the time we met, two former students of his – Paschal Donoghue and Philip Lane – were in the two most powerful financial positions in the State: Minister for Finance and head of the Central Bank, respectively. In the oldest building on the campus, dating from around 1700, he gave some very forward-looking analysis. 'I think immigration has been a win-win situation. It's led to a much more diverse population and it's led to an economic boom. We had a reversal of population for 150 years so as a longer-term objective we could aim for 10 million.' O'Hagan insists that we can avoid the mistake of the UK which ran down the health and education systems while the numbers were going up in the country. 'It's a function of good planning to provide the services for the population,' he said, pointing to the Netherlands as a good example.

The B-word

On the immediate horizon is the issue of Brexit. Part of the pain of Brexit for Ireland will be pulling away from the shared economic, political and cultural space with our neighbours when the British go their separate way. It is difficult to ignore the geographical fact that the island of Great Britain is sitting between us and the Continent.

Traditionally, the bulk of Ireland's exports to the continent have gone through Britain, the so-called landbridge. In October 2017, the MV Celine, the largest roll on/roll-off vessel in the world and twice the size of any other ferry operating out of Dublin Port, opened a service between Dublin and the ports of Zeebrugge in Belgium and Rotterdam in the Netherlands. The Luxembourg-based owners, CLdN, said the ship would provide additional capacity for customers trading with markets in continental Europe, 'particularly post-Brexit.' A new freight shipping route has also opened between Waterford Port and Rotterdam.

Boosting alternative routes is one option but what about all our trade across the Irish Sea? We have come a long way in overcoming our old dependency on our former ruler. From 98 per cent of exports at the birth of the State, just 11 per cent of total Irish exports were sold to the UK market in 2018, though the share for domestically-owned companies is much higher[xv] at 33 per cent.

That still makes the UK our biggest single European export destination (the US is top of the table with 28 per cent of exports). Along with economic and political ties comes the human connection. British nationals are one of Ireland's largest immigrant groups and vice versa. There are 400 flights a week between Dublin, Cork and Shannon and London. Trade is not the only thing depending on transit through Britain. That's also how we source more than 40 per cent of our energy needs in natural gas imports. And all this is not to mention the sensitive question of Northern Ireland and the border.

The UK and Ireland have always maintained a common travel area and special reciprocal rights for citizens. But it was largely thanks to shared membership of the Single Market and the peace dividend that the Irish border faded into insignificance, at least in terms of economic and social activity, if not in all hearts and minds.

It has been of great benefit to the economy of the island of Ireland to remove that obstacle to the free flow of goods, services and people. The absence of a hard border has given companies and communities the freedom to reach into their natural hinterland and develop healthily.

In his book *Brexit & Ireland*, Tony Connelly features Combilift, a forklift manufacturer in Gallinagh, in County Monaghan that encapsulates all of the challenges of Brexit.

'A quarter of its exports go to the UK, and the company is part of an elaborate supply chain involving dozens of small firms on both sides of the border.' The prospect of customs duties and/ or trade tariffs being introduced between the Republic and the North, not ruled out at the time of writing, would be disruptive, to put it mildly.

The Irish food industry, with 37 per cent of exports going to the UK, is the most exposed to Brexit, particularly because of the sensitivity of animal health regulations. With the island currently sharing the same health, safety and labelling regime, animals and meat currently move seamlessly back and forth across the border for slaughter and packaging. The same is true of milk and milk products. The Baileys Irish Cream supply chain alone generates about 5,000 border crossings a year of trucks carrying raw milk, cream, whiskey, bottles and corrugated paper, Connolly writes. Or take Silver Hill Farm in Monaghan, Ireland's biggest duck meat producer. Its eggs are laid over the border in Tyrone, hatched in County Monaghan and raised in farms north and south.

Quite apart from the danger of renewed political violence, reimposing a hard border on complex economic networks like this would be harmful.

But the change is not without opportunity. Being the only major English-speaking country left in the EU will be a nice advantage. The other 26 countries of the EU will become more important to us with the UK out of the picture. British companies with operations in the EU are well aware of Ireland's future usefulness. Barclays Bank, to name but one, has doubled its workforce in Dublin, expanding the office to a hub to run its European branch network and other activities.

Fresh thinking

These challenges are being taken very seriously by the Irish government whose Brexit team in the civil service is preparing as best it can for all eventualities. The Irish have been able to count on strong backing from the EU since the beginning of the negotiations.

Brexit will be the big distraction in the next few years, calling for huge resources and ingenuity. But this doesn't mean that the Irish economy shouldn't be subject to another kind of scrutiny. Economic growth does not happen in a vacuum. Economic policy has a major impact on the lives of individuals and should therefore be informed by some guiding principles. In the pursuit of growth above all and reverence for the market, Ireland has arguably lost sight of this responsibility. Almost 10,000 people living in emergency accommodation while rent prices rocket shows poor government planning at best and indifference at worst. The latest OECD economic survey found the Irish health system is failing in terms of cost, patient satisfaction and waiting times. The report recommends a move to universal coverage for primary healthcare, the lack of which contributes 'to poor access and high health costs for some households that cannot afford private insurance.'

These crucial questions on how will we house, educate and provide for the health of our people now and in the future need to be at the forefront of the debate. How far will we go to protect the environment? Ireland has been ranked worst in the EU for action on climate change. Ireland was also identified as the country that attracted the largest amount of shifted profits from multinationals avoiding tax (more than $100 billion in 2015). How long can we live with facilitating international tax avoidance on a massive scale? Vision is what's missing now. It is easy to mock the anti-materialism of the early decades of independence in the cold light of the success-driven 21st century but what has actually replaced it? What if we became 'the poster child for integrity'? Ethical investment funds already exist; Ireland is small enough to reinvent itself as the first ethical economy.

In a 2018 speech to the UCD School of Ethics, Irish president Michael D. Higgins put the challenge in these terms:

'As we stand at a highly critical juncture in world history, we must ask ourselves not merely what kind of society served by what kind of economy do we wish for Ireland, for the European Union of which we are a member, and for those living in vulnerable conditions across the globe. But more fundamentally, we must ask, is our scholarship, invoked so often as a source of policy, capable and willing to forge new connections of society, ethics, ecology and economy. The great intellectual challenges of our time depend for answers on that fundamental question.'[xvi]

Endnotes

---

[i] Source: Sweeney 1998, based on NESC (1990), and CSO Population and Migration Estimates (various years), cited in 'The Structural Failure of Irish Economic Development and Employment Policy' by Tom O'Connor, UCC, in the *Irish Journal of Public Policy*, Volume 2, Issue 2

[ii] 9th January 1980, televised address

[iii] 'Rich man, poor man, beggar man … ' by Justine McCarthy, *Irish Independent*, 13.02.1999

[iv] https://slate.com/culture/2006/03/the-faux-irish-pub-revolution.html

[v] https://www.ictu.ie/download/pdf/celtic_tiger.pdf

[vi] O'Hagan, John & O'Toole, Francis: *The Economy of Ireland*, Palgrave 2017, 13th edition, p. 27

[vii] https://www.rte.ie/news/2007/0704/90808-economy/

[viii] O'Toole, Fintan: *Ship of Fools: How stupidity and corruption sunk the Celtic Tiger*, Faber & Faber, 2009, p. 111

[ix] Evaluation of the Economic Adjustment Programme: Ireland, 2010 – 2013, Economic and Financial Affairs, European Commission, July 2015, PUB00356-025.

[x] Oireachtas Report of Joint Committee Inquiry into the banking crisis, Chapter 10

[xi] https://www.imf.org/en/News/Articles/2015/09/28/04/53/socar121913a

[xii] http://oecdobserver.org/news/fullstory.php/aid/5456/Ireland_92s_economy:_Still_riding_the_globalisation_wave.html

[xiii] IMD World Competitiveness Rankings 2019

[xiv] http://www.davidmcwilliams.ie/dont-worry-multinationals-are-not-about-to-up-sticks/

[xv] Enterprise Ireland figures for 2018, released 20.05.2019

[xvi] https://www.youtube.com/watch?v=zGF_Y7zJaNw

CHAPTER 9

The Irish hate the English

'From my earliest youth I have regarded the connection between Ireland and Great Britain as the curse of the Irish nation, and felt convinced, that while it lasted this country would never be free or happy.'

Theobald Wolfe Tone, addressing the court martial which later sentenced him to death, November 8, 1798

***

'The relationship between our two neighbouring nations is long, complex and has often been turbulent. Like the tides that surround each of us, we have shaped and altered each other. This evening we celebrate a new chapter in our relationship that may still be a work in progress, but happily, has also become a work of progress, of partnership and friendship.' [i]

President Mary McAleese addressing Queen Elizabeth II in Dublin Castle on the occasion of the British Queen's first State visit to Ireland after 59 years of being the British monarch, May 18, 2011

When I was growing up, we received occasional visits from our English cousins, children of my four uncles who had settled in the North of England. There was Jane who gave us all a fright when she nearly choked on a potato skin, and Michelle who was only ten but carried a handbag and talked non-stop. Our quiet cousin Kieran from Newcastle played under-16 squash for Ireland which meant we all got to see our first game of squash.

I remember liking these children but feeling a little sorry for them. The poor things, they had English accents. How sad it must be to have to grow up English, I thought. They had lost the most important thing about them.

One day two little cousins turned up at our house wearing the England soccer kit. It must have been a World Cup summer. As I watched the boys running around on the road in their white outfits, I was scandalised and embarrassed to the tips of my teenage ears. I had no appreciation for their different identity then. I just thought it was a travesty for an Irish child to be wearing the England colours. The fact that the boys' mother was English didn't lessen the offence. I had a long way to come.

The nationalist sentiment I was feeling was raw and sharp-edged. It stemmed from a solid conviction that the English were the bad guys and that the Irish, as victims of their badness, had earned a tacit superiority over them, the superiority of the victim. To bolster this view, any difference between the two nationalities was to be embraced, while similarities were to be glossed over. Only much later in life would I learn that the simplistic national pride I was feeling needed serious re-evaluation. It is the least helpful mindset for an English or Irish person to foster.

The problem is that it is very difficult as an Irish person to learn about the history of 'these islands' without developing some negative views of our neighbours. For most of history there was nothing benign in the relationship between the ruling English and the Irish. Pre-independence, it seems fair to say that the relationship was vexed, based on subjugation rather than any spirit of partnership. What the Irish wanted from the English was distance, more than the Irish Sea could ever provide. Likewise, the English may often have wished Ireland would just drift away into the Atlantic. But it is difficult for either party to move on as long as we are tied together by Northern Ireland. In that sense the past is not even past.

The eminent Irish historian J.J. Lee has no time for this kind of lament-driven analysis.

'It is usual to aver that the Irish are haunted by history, that they suffer from too much rather than too little historical consciousness. But the modern Irish, contrary to popular impression, have little sense of history. What they have is a sense of grievance, which they choose to dignify by christening it history.'[ii]

Bearing Lee's scolding words in mind, let's take a look at where that sense of grievance might come from.

The book of evidence

It used to be common to hear Irish people refer to 800 years of oppression, only sometimes in jest, when talking about the English. Why English and not British? Because the English, *na Sasanaigh*, were always the ones calling the shots, from the Irish point of view. It was the English language, English law and English kings and queens that were imposed on Ireland. The Scots and Welsh seemed like shadow nations, press-ganged into the United Kingdom to serve as enforcers.

The 800 years of English presence is soon to become 850 years, taking year zero as 1171, the date Henry II landed on the coast of Waterford, the first English King to come to Ireland. It was not

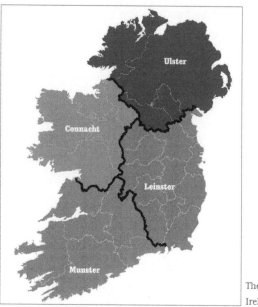

The four provinces of Ireland

a social visit. Henry travelled with a flotilla of more than 400 ships, an army of 5,000 soldiers and all the advanced military technology of the war-happy Normans. Henry had had his eye on Ireland for some time and had approved a Norman invasion two years beforehand.

In the prime of his life, 38-year-old Henry already ruled over England, half of modern-day France and much of Wales. By the end of his six-month stay in Ireland, without having to fight, he had established his authority over the Norman lords and some Gaelic princes, enough to control most of Leinster. The rest of the island, Henry II agreed to leave under the control of Rory O'Connor, then High King of Ireland.

And they all lived happily every after.

Only joking. The Norman lords and their descendants, with their superior castles and military might, could not resist the lure of conquest. They subdued one small kingdom after another until they held most of the country by 1300. The native Irish still held the western part of Ulster and parts of Connacht and Munster as well as pockets of territory in the midlands.

But by this stage the distinction between the two cultures had blurred. The Normans, known as the Old English, had intermarried with the Irish and adopted their customs and language. Two centuries of hands-off management by the English crown had allowed Irish society to continue to evolve in its own way, for example in the reliance on Brehon Law instead of English law.

When the clamp-down eventually came, in the form of the Statutes of Kilkenny (1367), it was strongly ethnically charged and set the approach that would be adhered to from then on. Fearful of its authority in Ireland being contaminated by the 'Irish enemies', the English crown insisted on separating the rulers from the ruled. The English were to live as a separate hostile nation in Ireland and the Irish would be subjugated, or else.

These punitive laws were not fully enforceable but they resonated down the centuries, and were echoed in the draconian Penal Laws against Catholics (mainly in the 18th century) which prevented the majority of the population from having a meaningful stake in society. At that stage religion had become the key marker to differentiate between the natives and the people in control. By the middle of the 18th century the proportion of land in Catholic ownership had shrunk to 3 per cent. The legacy of the statutes was very much in evidence in the Plantation of Ulster, and in the divergence of identity, rights and interests between the two communities in the area that became Northern Ireland.

It is bad for the soul to spend too much time dwelling on Irish history. Better not to think about Elizabeth I's lackeys in Ireland, testing out atrocities they would later use when colonising the

New World. Then we could forget men like Sir Walter Raleigh who was rewarded for his part in crushing the Second Desmond Rebellion with 40,000 acres in Counties Cork and Waterford. We could forget Oliver Cromwell's scorched earth policy a century later that reduced the population by a quarter, as well as the mass internal displacement this caused and the transportations into indentured servitude in the West Indies. We could draw a veil over the emasculating Act of Union, the inequities of land ownership and the evictions of the 19th century. We could block out the humanitarian disaster of the Great Famine, and we wouldn't have to rue the wasteful British mistake of denying Home Rule for 50 years until it was too late for the countries to separate peacefully.

Never mind. We all agree that a lot of regretful things happened which have overshadowed Irish independence and Anglo-Irish relations to the present day. But it must be remembered that the decisions taken in London with regard to Ireland were not taken in a vacuum. Local power struggles and opportunism on the island of Ireland had an influence, as did alliances and wars between England and other European powers. The unfortunate reality for the English, with so many different enemies over the centuries, was that they could not afford to leave Ireland unoccupied in case it might become a staging post for invasion. They were also constrained by the fear of Ireland providing a model for exiting the Empire. During the Irish War of Independence (1919-1921), the British controlled one quarter of the world's land surface and one fifth of the world's population.

Do the Irish hate the English? The short answer is no. What we do dislike is the simplistic kind of English nationalism which is still prevalent in contemporary politics and which is built on denial. In this version of reality, England is 'a proud nation that has repeatedly fought for freedom and liberty'.[iii] Ireland is and always was a thorn in England's side and the British Empire was primarily about 'spreading civilisation', so ultimately a force for good. Most importantly, in this version of history, Britain's role in the Second World War is everything. The honour, courage and endurance shown in those years are the defining characteristics of the nation.

It takes buckets of denial to believe that the expansion of the British Empire was about improving the lives of other peoples. It was about control – of territory, of labour and of resources – used to enforce a system of wealth extraction. It was based on a belief in the inferiority of other races and the idea that their lives and bodies were dispensable. The subjugation of the colonised people necessarily involved crimes against humanity, such as deliberate famines, massacres of civilians and concentration camps. And yet, a sizeable proportion of British people are proud of the history of colonialism. A YouGov survey in 2016 found that 44 per cent of respondents were proud of the Empire. Only 21 per cent said they regretted the Empire happened while 23 per cent held neither view. The percentage breakdown was similar for those who considered the British Empire a good thing (43 per cent), a bad thing (19 per cent) and neither good nor bad (25 per cent).

The Empire was the existential core of Britishness, itself an extension of Englishness, and the very antithesis of freedom. It left a sorry trail of death, exploitation and blighted societies around the world. Scores of nations had to fight for their freedom from the British right up to the 1970s. Many of those countries, from Afghanistan to Myanmar to Pakistan, are still experiencing conflict today not unrelated to their colonial history. Winning the Second World War with the help of the two budding superpowers, the US and the Soviet Union, does not change that record one whit.

To get back to Irish feelings towards the English, on a spectrum of negative to positive feelings, only a small cohort would feel strong animosity. Most are very comfortable with the people across the water and forgive them their ignorance in historical matters. After all, it is currently hurting them more than anyone else. The 103,000 British nationals living in Ireland are the country's second largest immigrant group after the Polish (122,515). We cannot read people's hearts or monitor every staff canteen but, as a general rule, anti-British sentiment is socially unacceptable. Watching some Brexit-promoting politicians veer close to self-parody in their efforts to beat the patriotic drum has provoked public and private scorn in Ireland. But it is firmly directed at the political opportunists in London, not ordinary people.

Still, the fundamentalist-style, angry Irish nationalists do walk among us. They are represented by the person or persons who threw paint on the statue of the Haunting Soldier, erected in St. Stephen's Green in Dublin to mark the centenary of the end of the First World War. If they desecrate the memory of the 49,000 Irishmen who were killed in the First World War just because those soldiers fought in the British Army, you can be sure they exist on an incoherent diet of anti-British hatred. For the rest of us, healing is the key, a tone set by most British and Irish leaders since the peace process began in the early 1990s. We recognise that each successive generation inherited a flawed relationship and a fraught situation. We can be grateful at what has been achieved in the current generation and we can aim higher so that we have something better to hand on to our children.

Help from across the waves

The fantasy of a European power coming to help Ireland in her hour of need goes back a long way, at least to the 1500s. At various times, Spanish and French armies and even some Papal troops landed on Irish shores to assist the Irish cause, temporarily raising hopes only to dash them again. There were other times when help was sought but not forthcoming, like the ill-fated Flight of the Earls in 1607. German help was sought in advance of the 1916 Rising – with little result.

So it is extremely gratifying for Ireland to currently have the full backing of the European Union in dealing with the crisis precipitated by the Brexit vote of June 2016. While it may seem obvious that a small member remaining in a club would take precedence over a big member leaving, neither the United Kingdom nor Ireland realised how firm this support would turn out to be.

The Irish government had a very clear position from the beginning, and their concerns were accepted by Brussels as legitimate. Those concerns centred on the future of the 500-kilometer border between the Republic of Ireland and Northern Ireland which is set to become an external border of the EU. More than 20 years of peace and 27 years of the Single Market have rendered the border virtually invisible against the background of a shared, non-contentious, third identity of being European. The political, social and economic dividend of this change cannot be underestimated. The fact that the implications for Ireland were given so little consideration in the Brexit debate speaks volumes about the level of interest and knowledge in British politics.

So it was that a satisfactory solution for the Irish border became one of the three points to be settled at Brussels' insistence during the Withdrawal Agreement negotiations. The issue would not be set aside for a later stage, as the UK wanted. The other two points were the rights of EU citizens resident in the UK and the settlement of what was owed by the UK, the so-called divorce bill. The

Withdrawal Agreement, the result of 18 months of negotiations, was published in November 2018. It has been accepted by the 27 other members of the EU but faced difficulties securing enough votes for ratification in Westminster. In the agreement, British negotiators accepted a 'backstop' to resolve the border question, essentially a guarantee that no arrangement would be introduced that would create a hard border – physical checks or infrastructure – on the island of Ireland. The UK-wide backstop, if activated, is only meant to be in place 'unless and until' better solutions can be found.

While the EU backing has been good for Irish interests and self-esteem, the strength of the Irish position has angered some elements of the British media and political class who have accused the Irish government of acting in bad faith, weaponising Brexit to achieve a united Ireland. The Irish Ambassador to the United Kingdom was provoked to write to *The Spectator* magazine in April 2019 to complain of the 'snide and hostile' tone used in articles about Ireland.

None of these strains have been helped by the fact the then Prime Minister Teresa May had to rely on the 10 MPs of Northern Ireland's Democratic Unionist Party (DUP) to prop up her government throughout the Brexit negotiations. The socially-regressive DUP, acting contrary to the wishes of the majority of Northern Irish voters who rejected Brexit, is the least sympathetic to the interests of the Republic of Ireland, even when those interests coincide with the interests of Northern Ireland[iv]. Shamefully, Northern Ireland's power-sharing executive, set up in 1999, which should have been providing leadership in Northern Ireland at this crucial time, is no use, since it collapsed amidst mutual recrimination in January 2017.

The current frustrations are a far cry from the positive

atmosphere that surrounded the Good Friday Agreement of 1998, made viable by common membership of the EU. A year earlier, the then newly-elected Prime Minister Tony Blair even apologised for the British role in the Great Famine, the first British leader to address the catastrophe. In a letter read out during a festival in County Cork to commemorate the Famine, Blair said:

'The famine was a defining event in the history of Ireland and Britain. It has left deep scars. That one million people should have died in what was then part of the richest and most powerful nation in the world is something that still causes pain as we reflect on it today. Those who governed in London at the time failed their people.'[v]

In 2007, a huge psychological barrier was broken when the British national anthem was played in Croke Park at the beginning of a Six Nations rugby match between Ireland and England. The north Dublin venue is hallowed in nationalist lore, not just for the sports played there but because it was the scene of a massacre of civilians by security forces during the War of Independence. The decision by the Gaelic Athletic Association (GAA) to change its rule

Queen Elizabeth II, with President Mary McAleese, prepares to lay a wreath in the Garden of Remembrance, Dublin, 2011.

banning the playing of so-called garrison games (rugby, soccer and field hockey) in its stadiums was widely welcomed in Ireland. The home side won the match 43-13.

When Queen Elizabeth II visited Ireland in 2011, the first official visit of her 59-year reign, she visited the Garden of Remembrance and laid a wreath there in honour of those who fought against Britain for Irish independence. This was another powerfully symbolic moment. In her speech at Dublin Castle she referred to the two countries as 'firm friends and equal partners'.

Parting ways

While we are speaking about the hard-won friendship between Ireland and the UK, there is more to unpick about what the European Union has done for the relationship. On a visit to Dublin in 2018, John Major gave a speech to the Institute of International and European Affairs in which he reminisced fondly about the European connection. He said there was a time when Irish and British ministers met only rarely and then to disagree. The EU changed that.

'Europe was where I first met [his Irish counterpart] Albert Reynolds, it was where we became friends, it was where we learnt to trust one another. But no longer [after Brexit] will Irish and British ministers be able to meet and speak there privately and productively for their joint interests.'

Major described the loss of contact as unquantifiable but profound. 'The two sides will no longer be able to bond over common causes in Europe.'

There is a consensus on this view, as expressed by President Mary McAleese during Queen Elizabeth's visit, before Brexit took over British politics. 'The collegial and cooperative relationship between the British and Irish Governments was crucial to the success of the Peace Process and we can thank the deepening engagement between us as equal partners in the European Union for the growth of friendship and trust.'

The United Kingdom is going through the biggest crisis it has faced since the Second World War. Ireland is the EU country most affected by that crisis, which is driven by a resurgence in raw British nationalism infused with Empire nostalgia. Not only is the UK's economy and place in the world thrown into doubt, but a question mark also hangs over the union with Scotland and with Northern Ireland.

The EU grew from a group of 6 countries to a group of 28 over more than 60 years. The UK was on board for 43 years (until the Brexit vote) of that process, along with Ireland, and was a key architect and proponent of the Single Market which came into being in 1993. To date, no country has left the EU. Other European countries which are not members cultivate very close relations with the EU, either through the European Economic Area package or through tailor-made alignment with the Single Market, customs union and/or the Schengen Agreement.

So leaving the EU is a new concept but it is imaginable, assuming you approach the task with good planning and goodwill for the rest of the union. That we are where we are today clearly shows the plan had no great minds or vision behind it. A hugely risky and complex process – diplomatically, economically, socially – was falsely sold as an easy proposition. One of a myriad of reasons for which 52 per cent of voters decided to vote Leave.

The goal, or the game, was to stir up as much discontent as possible while using the debate as a vessel for grand-standing and disruption. At the end of it all, the Leave campaign has left us with a dated, mean-spirited brand of nationalism in lieu of a workable roadmap for Brexit. The English and Welsh decision to leave the EU, dragging Scotland and Northern Ireland along, was based on negative, not to mention dishonest, campaigning. The narrative of the European Union as a tyrannous force from which the British have to be liberated is bizarre considering the UK's influential place in the union and the special exceptions it successfully negotiated over the years.

Three years after the vote, at the time of writing, the British parliament still could not find a form of Brexit to agree on. For the Irish, there is too much at stake for schadenfreude. The dominant feeling is disbelief that we are witnessing such an extreme public display of incompetence and bad judgment on the part of our former rulers. Whatever we thought of the English, we never considered them to be foolish.

The British rejection of the EU, adopting the role of the thankless child, has brought the rest of the family closer together – for now. But the long-term effects are impossible to predict. Nobody wants the population of the UK to go through undue suffering and instability. What's bad for them is bad for us too. We also want to contain the instability that is already emerging, especially in this age of intolerant nationalism where democracy is under threat and consensus politics is no longer the norm.

The EU has plenty of shortcomings and often does not live up to its own ideals, but we don't know what life in Europe would be like without it. When it comes to regional trade, the EU is the only game in town. When it comes to geopolitical influence, 28 countries may find it hard to reach consensus, but as a group they still manage to play an important role as a global voice for democracy. How the Irish and British will operate on either side of that divide in the future is hard to imagine. We will be shaking our heads for years at the folly and fallout of Brexit on Ireland. We will have to be forgiving.

The same but different

A 'West Brit' is a derogatory term for an Irish person who acts English, be it in accent, cultural tastes or politics. It is still used as an insult, a reminder of how essential it is to Irish identity that we are different from the English. Otherwise what was it all for?

One man who made it his life's work to enhance Irish identity was Eamon de Valera. A commander of the 1916 Easter Rising, he became the most dominant personality in 20th century Irish politics in a career that encompassed seven decades up to the 1970s. The grandfather of the nation, he finished his second term as president at the age of 90! Such was his influence that children were still playing a skipping game to the rhyme 'Vote, vote, vote for de Valera' in my national school in the 1980s.

De Valera had very clear, uncompromising ideas about Irish identity. He was a staunch Catholic and saw Catholicism as a crucial point of differentiation between Ireland and England. Today, the religion of the majority still links Ireland to a global community of nations that does not include England.[vi] 'The Long Fellow' rejected the materialism and loose morals that went along with industrialised societies and dreamed of a purer and simpler rural destiny for Ireland, hence his fondness for censoring films and books. Pride in Ireland's supposedly glorious past before English involvement was another recurring theme, and de Valera did his utmost to boost the Gaelic culture, particularly the language. The past, presented by de Valera as a story of oppression and persecution, was also a way of highlighting the difference between Ireland and England.

For a taste of de Valera's rhetoric, how about his response to Winston Churchill after the British leader criticised Ireland's wartime neutrality in a radio broadcast at the end of the Second World War. De Valera waited a few days before responding in his own broadcast from Dublin on May 17, 1945.

'Mr. Churchill is proud of Britain's stand alone, after France had fallen and before America entered the War. Could he not find in his heart the generosity to acknowledge that there is a small nation that stood alone not for one year or two, but for several hundred years against aggression; that endured spoliations, famines, massacres in endless succession; that was clubbed many times into insensibility, but that each time on returning consciousness took up the fight anew; a small nation that could never be got to accept defeat and has never surrendered her soul?'

The Irish language policy may not have been a great success, but Gaelic games, out of the hands of the State, became hugely popular, what sociologist Katie Liston calls 'the dominant marker of Irish cultural identity and difference'.[vii]

With 2,200 clubs in the 32 counties, the GAA is unique, 'stitched inexorably into family, community and parish life like no other sporting or cultural organisation'. Second only to the Catholic Church in its heyday, with the difference being that the heyday of the GAA is now. The GAA has also turned out to be a great vehicle for integration, welcoming people of all nationalities and religions with a proactive inclusion policy.

Historically, there was one nation that was excluded. 'From its inception, through its formal rules of membership, it also embodied an explicit opposition to British cultural imperialism,' Liston explains. Up until 1971, members were prohibited from 'participating in those sports most closely associated with British colonialism', among them – rugby union, association football (soccer) and hockey. Those barriers are gone, and probably forgotten, by young sportsmen and women today.

Nowadays we share a lot of cultural space with the British, though the traffic of content is still largely one-way. The Irish love affair with British football teams is obviously unrequited. You won't catch any English people travelling to Ireland to see Dundalk FC. No, we watch their television channels and shop in their shops. Irish consumers cannot get enough of British high street stores and supermarkets. We even read British newspapers, either the originals or the Irish editions.

The hype over the John Lewis Christmas advert shows how far things have gone. John Lewis & Partners is an iconic British chain of department stores which dates back to 1864 in Oxford Street, London. You might not ever have set foot in a John Lewis store, but you will probably know its sentimental Christmas adverts which have gone viral in recent years. The brand is famous for this annual advert, which is a marketeer's dream and now a much-anticipated fixture in British culture even though it's only been running since 2007.

There are 51 John Lewis stores in England, Scotland and Wales and one concession inside Arnott's department store in Dublin city centre, opened in 2016. Safe to say, John Lewis as a business does not play an important role in Ireland.

And yet, John Lewis plays a big role in British culture, which means Irish people are interested and aware of it. It also means that the Irish media do not want Irish readers to click on British websites for their first viewing of the ad. Which is why Irish news outlets – from the most serious to the most frivolous – are all over the launch of the ad. This virtual closeness is backed up by the Common Travel Area which amounts to a freedom of movement deal between the two countries. More than 400 flights a week leave Irish airports for London alone. [viii]

There is no denying the English imprint on Ireland. We speak the same language. Our cities and towns are graced by British architecture and we have various legacies of the British administration, from the legal system to separate taps for hot and cold. As the success of Irish comedians in Britain shows, we get each other's humour just as we like the same food. There has been so much traipsing back and forth between the two islands that we also share a lot of DNA. Irish nationals are the third-largest immigrant group in the UK (350,000 people[ix]) and the number of British nationals of Irish descent applying for Irish passports has reached tens of thousands per month in the aftermath of Brexit.

It is my hope that any cooling in sympathy between the two nations provoked by Brexit will be temporary and skin deep. We have too much in common and there is too much at stake for either side to slip back into an attitude of suspicion and recrimination. Been there, done that. But difficult times do lie ahead, especially if the 'precious union' begins to unravel. Elizabeth Bowen once wrote, 'England and Ireland each turned to the other a closed, harsh, distorted face – a face that, in each case, their lovers would hardly know.'[x] We cannot let that happen again.

In focus: Pat Jourdan, a fish into water

English-born writer Pat Jourdan thought of herself as Liverpool Irish, even though her family had lived for more than a century in England. 'My mother was always talking about Ireland. It became a sort of hunger.' In her fifties, after getting divorced and inheriting some money, she finally felt free to move to Ireland in 1995 and bought a shop in Galway which she renamed Ó *Maidin go hOíche* (From Morning 'Til Night).

'This shop was going to save the world. Two of the main assistants spoke Irish and I had everything labelled in Irish, like *arán* for bread. I had as much stock made in Ireland as possible, Irish greeting cards and an Irish dictionary behind the till.'

She described coming to live in Ireland as like a fish getting back into water. There was one detail that might have been problematic. She had a son serving in the British Army in Northern Ireland at the time. 'My idea was to tell everyone about that so the news spread out. Nobody gave a damn.'

Jourdan joined the writing scene in Galway at a time when there were countless events and gatherings. 'You could do this seven nights a week. It was wonderful and free and it was friendly. Later it got to be monetised.' She started to have some success with her short stories.

'For the first years Galway still felt like a village. People invited me into their homes. Come and have a cup of tea, Pat. I got talking to a woman one day who was polishing the brass on a front door. It turned out she didn't live on our street, she just liked going along polishing people's doorknobs. She couldn't write very well and I helped her write some letters after that, to do with a dispute in her family. She would have angry things to say but I toned it down.'

'I got involved with a local Green Party candidate and went around canvassing. At one house a woman was very nasty. You're not one of us, she said.'

'And there were a couple of times where people went on at me about the Famine or the 800 years of English oppression. It was me who was a famine victim! That's why my family left. But being involved with the shop, and the writing and being Catholic, I sort of blended in.'

Liverpool-Irish
My father endured the taunts of 'tick'
(from a man called Keenan) and bore
the nickname 'Paddy' uneasily;
yet would stiffen to the reel
 and set his jaw for the camera.

He would laugh at the Pier head Irish,
gazing out beyond the river's foggy mouth
to a neglectful motherland, through eyes
distant in drink and false memory;
doing the math on the rounds and neatly

balancing their cost against that to re-buy
the family farm. Yet he was in clover
to hear his name in *The Irish Rover*
and talked of cousins in Wicklow
with the requisite exile's glow.

The celtic *mestizo* thing is awkward.
Fit to be called diaspora, commodified
in song, yet welcomed back but slowly,
when we've stayed away too long: history's
tenant cousins twice-removed.

I was once suspect enough for passport
stamps, *MON DROIT* and my name to keep me
all day in Holyhead for routine questions.
but my accent's enough still to Cromwell our pitch
in some *gaeltacht* pub in Ballynahinch[xi]

Martin Malone, *The Waiting Hillside*

Endnotes

[i] Remarks made by President McAleese at the State dinner in honour of Queen Elizabeth II in Dublin Castle, 18.05.2011

[ii] Lee, J.J., *Ireland 1912 - 1985: Politics and Society*, Cambridge University Press, 1989, Preface, p. xiv

[iii] https://www.opendemocracy.net/en/opendemocracyuk/i-was-strong-brexiteer-now-we-must-swallow-our-pride-and-think-again/

[iv] It was the DUP who shot down the suggestion of a Northern-Ireland-only backstop.

[v] Blair Issues Apology for Irish Potato Famine, *The Independent*, 02.06.1997

[vi] *History Ireland*, Issue 2 (Summer 1997), Volume 5

[vii] *Are the Irish Different?* edited by Tom Inglis, Manchester University Press, 2004, Chapter: The GAA and the Sporting Irish by Katie Liston, p.200

[viii] IDA Facts about Ireland, November 2018

[ix] 2017 figures from the Migration Observatory, Oxford University

[x] From *Bowen's Court* (1942) by Elizabeth Bowen

[xi] Malone, Martin, *The Waiting Hillside*, Templar Poetry, 2011

CHAPTER 10

The Irish are Friendly

'When Irish eyes are smiling, sure 'tis like a morn in spring.
In the lilt of Irish laughter, you can hear the angels sing.
When Irish hearts are happy, all the world seems bright and gay,
And when Irish eyes are smiling, sure, they steal your heart away.'

When Irish Eyes are Smiling, lyrics by Chauncey Olcott
and George Graff (1912)

What do the Rhine Falls in Switzerland, the Victoria Falls in Zambia and the world's tallest building, the Burj Khalifa in Dubai, have in common? They are among more than 400 global landmarks that were lit up green for St Patrick's Day in 2019, the tenth year of the Global Greening campaign.

It is very nice of other countries to join the celebrations of our national day but isn't it also a little bit odd? No other country is using its national day and colour in the same way as the Irish. No other country would get away with it.

St Patrick's Day was traditionally a muted occasion in Ireland, a holy day of obligation when people wore a sprig of fresh shamrock on their coats and braved the (almost guaranteed) bad weather to go to Mass. Pubs were closed on March 17 until 1973. Famously, the only place you could get a drink on St Patrick's Day in Dublin back then was at the annual Dog Show, a well-attended event by all accounts.

The Irish Americans were the first to mark St Patrick's Day with parades, from as early as the mid-1700s, a tradition which was eventually copied in Ireland on a smaller scale. As time went on, the American version of St Patrick's Day became bigger and brasher, with a propensity for dyeing things green. For more than 50 years, Chicago river has turned green for the occasion, an idea that seemed extraordinary and a bit hysterical to the Irish on this side of the Atlantic, pre-Celtic Tiger.

But since the creation in 1996 of Dublin's St Patrick's Festival, celebrations in the Irish capital have been transformed into a glittering five-day production. The event is worth €73 million to the economy, attracting more than 100,000 visitors from abroad.[i] The city and town parades in the rest of the country have also grown in size and stature, as have the parades around the world.

The Global Greening campaign is an extension of this upscaling. Thanks to an Irish charm offensive, countries have volunteered their national monuments, from the Christ the Redeemer Statue above Rio de Janeiro to the Great Wall of China, to take part in something far removed from their own culture. The people doing the charming are the diplomats of the Irish embassy network and employees of Tourism Ireland.

The campaign, which started with just one landmark, Sydney Opera House in 2010, now has a life of its own. Representatives of the various cultural sites increasingly approach the organisers, asking to take part. Images of the buildings and landmarks bathed in green light are widely published, creating a win-win publicity buzz.

This substantial goodwill towards Ireland, the country that is everybody's friend, also feeds into Irish success in courting foreign direct investment (FDI), work carried out by the State's inward investment promotion agency, IDA Ireland. An estimated one in five private sector jobs is directly or indirectly attributable to FDI.

So what makes the Irish adept at soft power? Of course it helps that Ireland is 'harmless' in military and economic terms. Better than that, Ireland has consistently done well in the Good Country Index[ii] (currently in third place), which ranks countries on the basis of their contribution to the greater good of humanity. The index uses data from the United Nations and other international organisations to measure how well countries advance the interests of people in other countries, not just their own. Ireland scores well in cultural influence and its contribution to international peace and security, health and wellbeing.

That official Ireland is very friendly is very much in keeping with the unofficial national personality. We know the Irish are friendly because tourists keep telling us that. Three Irish cities – Cork, Galway and Dublin – made it into the top 10 of the friendliest cities in the world in the 2018 Condé Nast traveller survey.

Selective welcome

From Heinrich Böll's *Irish Journal* (1957) to Tony Hawk's *Round Ireland with a Fridge* (1998), travel writing about Ireland always emphasises the warm welcome extended to travellers, and the friendliness of the people. In Fáilte Ireland's 2016 survey, 99 per cent of respondents were very satisfied with both the hospitality and friendliness of the people.[iii] The warm reception they received ranks above everything else, even the scenery.

This is a particular type of friendliness we are talking about – short term, no commitment, and overwhelmingly involving white visitors. It may be accompanied by a genuine desire to connect or it may simply be a reflex reaction to a certain category of stranger. Not everyone is treated to *céad míle fáilte*[iv] in Ireland.

Tony Hawk and his fridge on their journey around Ireland

There is a wonderful radio documentary about a Dubliner, Dick Tynan, who served in the US army in the 1950s, and befriended an African American man, Private Howard Branch. It begins as a really sweet story. The two young men were stationed together in Germany and got on well, sharing a passion for jazz. But their friendship wasn't to last. One day, when Dick mentioned he was going home to Dublin on leave, Howard dropped a hint that he would be interested in coming along. Dick hesitated and Howard misinterpreted his reluctance as a sign that Dick didn't want him to come because he was black.

That was the reason, but not in the way Howard thought. Dick grew up in inner city Dublin and had witnessed black people, mainly medical students in those days, being horribly racially abused in the street. He didn't trust his fellow Dubliners and was afraid of that happening to Howard.

The issue was too tricky for Dick to explain and, sadly, led to a coolness between the men. Then, a short time afterwards, Howard was killed in a road accident, in which Dick was also injured. Dick blamed himself because he had made room in the back of the truck for Howard at the last minute. He was traumatised for years by this mixture of guilt about the accident and about the misunderstanding that ended his friendship with Howard. The story, *Finding Private Branch,* is very sensitively told, mostly in Dick's voice, in the documentary made by his daughter Mary Elaine Tynan.[v]

Turning to the present day, I spoke to Joy, a long-time Irish resident from Zimbabwe, now a naturalised Irish citizen. Joy and I have a lot in common. We are both professional women who have lived away from our countries of origin for the same amount of time, and our children are around the same ages. Yet, our experiences of immigrant life are worlds apart, for the simple reason that Joy is black.

The European Commission against Racism and Intolerance (ECRI), established by the Council of Europe, reports on racism and discrimination in Ireland.[vi] In its latest report it observed that hate speech involving verbal abuse in public places is quite common. 'There is an undercurrent of low-level racist violence which is not adequately recorded or addressed,' the report said.

Joy can attest to that. Joy came to Ireland legally from Zimbabwe as a young woman, full of hope and self-confidence. She had a work permit, a career plan and an idea that the Irish were a compassionate people. In her first week in Dublin a woman spat at her on the street and shouted racial abuse.

'When someone spits at you, they are showing their disgust for you. They are showing that you are less than human to them. What it does is it degrades you. It plays havoc with your mind and identity.'

Racism became a fixture in Joy's life, shattering her trust in Irish society. This is not a triumph-over-adversity story. The adversity is not over; it may never be. And now Joy worries about her children's future.

'Since then, there have been so many incidents. When it happens, people just stand and look. Saying nothing says something. I have reported five incidents of racial crimes to the Gardaí, but there was never any follow-up and action. I cannot keep asking and trying [for justice]. Otherwise this thing, this othering, will have a constant hold over my life.'

Ireland has not renewed its National Action Plan against Racism which ended in 2008. The ECRI has also complained that there are no provisions in Irish law defining common offences of a racist nature as specific offences, 'nor any specific or statutory provision for racist or other hate motivation to be considered as an aggravating circumstance for all criminal offences'.

Apart from violent, aggressive incidents, Joy has been confronted with subtle forms of racism as well as institutional racism, especially in the jobs market. 'Once I went through the recruitment process for a job in a leading Irish company, and after the phone interview I was told I was the only candidate being considered. I was asked to come in for a final interview. The receptionist was very rude to me, asking me in a hostile tone what I was doing there. It was immediately clear to me that they were not expecting a black person. They must have assumed from my accent that I was a white African. The first question the interviewers asked was "why is your accent not African?" As if I had tricked them. The interview went downhill from there.'

The authorities do not make it easier. Joy's mother, a full-time teacher, could not get a visa to visit Ireland when Joy got married, and not even when Joy was critically ill. After many years of trying, she was finally granted a visa to visit Ireland with supporting letters from the third level institution Joy graduated from.

When Joy had black friends visiting from the US, Netherlands,

France and Canada, they all separately had negative interactions based on their race. Joy cannot bring herself to invite them again. What a terrible indictment of Irish social progress that the worries felt by an Irishman in 1959 about his soldier friend would still be felt 60 years later.

The interview I did with Joy was one of the saddest I have ever done because there was so much pain in her voice and no apparent solution to her plight. 'This whole reality of being a black woman living in Ireland has isolated me,' she said.

Irish population by ethnicity 2016		%
White Irish	3,854,266	82.18
Any other white background	446,727	9.52
Asian or Asian Irish – Chinese	19,447	0.41
Asian or Asian Irish of any other Asian background	79,273	1.69
Black or Black Irish – African	57,850	1.23
Black or Black Irish – any other black background	6,879	0.14
Other including mixed background	70,603	1.5
Traveller	30,907	0.66
Not stated	124,019	2.64

Census 2016 (percentages are 0.03 per cent short of 100% because of rounding)

Irish society is still at least 92 per cent white[vii], while the black population is below 1.5 per cent. The hostile cohort of Irish racists creates problems for black citizens, residents and visitors trying to go about their daily business in Ireland. The EU Agency for Fundamental Rights found that 51 per cent of people of African descent had experienced hate-motivated harassment in Ireland, compared to 21 per cent in the UK.[viii] Ireland was among the worst in the EU for violence based on skin colour.

That lack of inhibition or any kind of shame, coupled with hateful attitudes, produces overt racism which is an ugly side to Irish society. It is the other side of the coin to the celebrated nice behaviour of the Irish, which is also expressed without inhibition. Fringe elements in politics, who have had little to no success at the ballot box, have been trying to whip up anti-immigrant sentiment, targeted at anyone who is a shade darker than Irish pale. They have a small following, but they are active on social media and in real life to an extent, finding support and echo from ethno-nationalist movements in other parts of Europe and the US. According to the ECRI, the Prohibition of Incitement to Hatred Act 1989 'is seldom used and is particularly ineffectual in combating online hate speech.'

The other failing of the State is the overreliance on the direct provision system, under which asylum seekers are housed indefinitely in hostel-style accommodation and are given only a small allowance for incidental expenses. The ECRI report also called this out. It is directly related to problems with racism, as residents of these accommodation centres become easy targets.

'Direct provision accommodation for asylum seekers and refugees continues to present major concerns, including length of stay, overcrowding, inability to conduct normal family life, and harassment and threats experienced by LGBT asylum seekers,' the report said.

For the residents, direct provision is like being in an abusive relationship, writes Melatu Uche Okorie in her book, *This Hostel Life*. The author came to Ireland from Nigeria and spent more than eight years in the direct provision system. In one of her stories, the main character endures name calling in the street, men soliciting sex from her and security men following her around shops. 'I wanted to highlight the everyday racism that most African people living in Ireland who I've had conversations with have faced,'[ix] Okorie writes in the introduction to the book.

Our reputation for welcoming visitors is something to be proud of, and there are many encouraging tales about the welcome and acceptance shown to immigrants, but any honest discussion of Irish friendliness must address this shameful hole in the welcome mat.

Circles of belonging

To grow up in Ireland is to grow up with blanket permission to speak. When you are involved in a social interaction or a shared situation, however minor, you are free to speak to the other person in a friendly, informal way. Often it is more than permission, it is an expectation, a way of acknowledging the common ground between you. The subtext is, I know you already, we are just double checking that.

In a longer interaction, permission to speak moves to a different phase – permission to dig out a connection. Then you know where to place the person in your circles of belonging. There can be a slightly craven touch to this communication, because of the importance of being liked.

This has a lot to do with social codes in Ireland that favour relationships over rules. In her book, *Rule-Breakers – Why 'Being There' Trumps 'Being Fair' in Ireland*, sociologist Niamh Hourigan explores in depth the combination of weak rules and strong relationships that are a feature of Irish society, largely due to colonialism. Excluded from decision-making power or other forms of power, people exerted influence and sought support through unofficial networks, from family outwards.

Despite the top-down ruling systems that have developed through the modernisation of society and the economy since the 1960s, 'a relationship-based vision of good behaviour has continued to be an important part of the Irish value system', according to Hourigan. This was one of the explanations for the free-for-all that developed in the Irish economy in the lead-up to the 2008 financial crisis. No-one in the financial or governing elite, from ministers, to bankers, to regulators, was able to take the necessary steps to bring the Irish property market back into a sensible zone – in large part because of the connections they shared.

This cultivation of relationships operates at all levels of society, people doing each other favours, attending funerals, looking out for each other – and if necessary, bending the rules.

'Irish people are inclined to see rules as inherently unfair and operating in favour of elites ... As a consequence, an intimacy or relationship-based vision of good behaviour which stresses the importance of "being there" for others in circles of intimacy (groups often described as "our own") has dominated ... This intimacy lies at the heart of the celebrated warmth and friendliness of Irish culture. It also lies at the core of every corruption scandal since the 1960s ...', Hourigan writes.

In terms of how we view ourselves, in real life conversation and on social media, it is telling what anecdotes or situations are used to confirm various perceptions about Irishness. The 'onlyin Ireland' hashtag reveals the three main stereotypes that are embraced. In the first and most prevalent, people share scenes or situations that illustrate Irish people's informality or spontaneity, things like two male politicians waltzing together for fun in parliament or kids playing an impromptu traditional music session on a plane. The second main type of behaviour that prompts people to say 'only in Ireland' is in instances of incompetence or stupidity, such as mistaken road markings, and the final category is the rural idyll, images of farm animals or beautiful, empty beaches. The pinnacle of the latter category would be a flock of sheep or cows blocking the road, with the caption 'Irish traffic jam'.

'My friend Clare'

My own 'only in Ireland' story involves two funerals and is as good a place as any to bring this book to a close. Funerals are big occasions in Ireland, in public and private life. The media coverage of tragic deaths includes live reporting of the victims' funerals. But even outside the news cycle, funerals are important, well-attended community occasions. They are an opportunity for everyone connected to every member of the bereaved family, not just the deceased person, to show they care. The best compliment to the deceased is to be able to say that there was a big crowd in the church.

When I got the news that my uncle Michael had died in October 2017, my first thought was to figure out how I could attend the funeral. I rejigged my childcare and managed to find a flight that would get me to Dublin in time for the removal, on the eve of the funeral.

As it happened, my train to Geneva was delayed and I arrived at the airport station at the time I should have been boarding. I decided to make a run for it, in the hope that boarding would be delayed. Twenty minutes' later I skidded into the departure area, a panting, dishevelled mess, just in time to see the air bridge disconnect from the plane. The ground staff at the gate shrugged their shoulders. There was nothing they could do for me.

So I sat down and tried to get my breath back, willing the tears not to come. A minute after me, another woman made an equally frantic entrance. I watched as she came and appealed to the same staff about the same flight. She was Irish too and we had apparently been on the same delayed train.

I did the most natural thing in the world for an Irishwoman: I spoke to her. She came and sat down next to me and we compared notes on the train delay, the decision to run for it, the frustration of being able to see the plane but not board it.

'And the awful thing is,' I said, 'I'm on my way to my uncle's funeral.'

She looked amazed. 'I'm on my way to my uncle's funeral too!'

'Really? It's my uncle Michael. The removal is tonight.'

'What? It's my uncle Michael, too! And the removal is tonight.'

Had I discovered a long-lost cousin? No, we quickly established that there were two uncle Michaels being buried in two different parts of Dublin the next day. What happened next fits into Irish cultural norms: Liz and I joined forces. We both wanted to get the next available flight to Dublin which meant having to spend the night in one of the world's most expensive cities. First, we considered sharing a hotel room but the prices were so high. Then Liz thought of someone she might be able to ask for a bed for the night, the ex-wife of a cousin. So, she gave her a call.

'I'm at the airport with my friend Clare,' she began, winking at me. And that is how I ended up sharing a sofa bed with someone I had just met, in an apartment full of Charles and Di memorabilia. We shared a taxi to the airport at five the next morning and we both made it home on time for our respective funerals.

Even though we didn't keep in touch afterwards, meeting Liz in these circumstances was a lovely, heart-warming experience. It was an example of the Irish desire to seek a connection with a stranger, some common ground, and when that connection was stronger than expected, to be instantly willing to throw in our lot together. As Ireland becomes more diverse, and young people from different backgrounds are educated, play and work together, the circles of belonging are changing to reflect that mix. The only Irish people who should be feeling isolated in this day and age are those who put others at risk by spreading hate and hurt.

Endnotes

---

[i] 'Plan to turn St Patrick's Day into month-long shindig', by Deirdre Falvey, *The Irish Times*, 12.2.2019

[ii] Established by Simon Anholt in 2014

[iii] Overseas holidaymakers' attitudes survey, Main markets 2016, based on interviews with 1,996 overseas tourists.

[iv] Traditional phrase of welcome meaning 'a hundred thousand welcomes'

[v] Documentary on One, *Finding Private Branch*, 29.09.18, RTÉ Radio One

[vi] ECRI fifth country monitoring report on Ireland, published 04.06.2019

[vii] Census of population 2016

[viii] https://fra.europa.eu/sites/default/files/fra_uploads/fra-2018-being-black-in-the-eu_en.pdf

[ix] Okerie, Melatu Uche, *This Hostel Life*, Skein Press, 2018, page iv, Author's Note

Akenson, DH, *If the Irish Ran the World: Montserrat 1630-1730* (Liverpool University Press, 1997).

Allen, Kieran, *Ireland's Economic Crash: A Radical Agenda for Change* (The Liffey Press, 2009)

Boland, Eavan, *Object Lessons: The Life of the Woman and the Poet in Our Time* (Carcanet Press, 1995)

Böll, Heinrich (translated by Leila Vennewitz), *Irish Journal* (Melville House Publishing, 2011, originally published in German as *Irisches Tagebuch* in 1957 by Verlag Kipenheuer & Witsch)

Carswell, Simon, *Anglo Republic: Inside the Bank that Broke Ireland* (Penguin, 2011)

Connolly, Tony, *Brexit & Ireland: The Dangers, the Opportunities and the Inside Story of the Irish Response* (Penguin Ireland, 2016)

Cruise O'Brien, Máire, *The Same Age as the State* (The O'Brien Press, 2003)

Cullen Owens, Rosemary, *A Social History of Women in Ireland: 1870 to 1970* (Gill & Macmillan, 2005)

D'Alton, Ian & Milne, Ida, *Protestant and Irish, The minority's search for place in independent Ireland* (Cork University Press, 2019)

Deane, Seamus, *Strange country: Modernity and Nationhood in Irish Writing since 1790* (Clarendon Press, 1999)

Dillon, Myles, *Early Irish Literature* (Four Courts Press, 1994)

Donoghue, Denis, *We Irish* (Alfred A. Knopf, 1986)

Findlay, Ronald and O'Rourke, Kevin H., *Power and Plenty: Trade, War, and the World Economy in the Second Millennium* (Princeton University Press, 2009)

Finnegan, Richard B and McCarron Edward T., *Ireland: Historical Echoes, Contemporary Politics* (Westview Press, 2000)

Foster, R.F., *The Irish Story: Telling Tales and Making it Up in Ireland* (Allen Lane, The Penguin Press, 2001)

Foster, R.F., *Luck and the Irish: A Brief History of Change, 1970-2000* (Penguin Books, 2008)

Foster, R.F., *Modern Ireland 1600-1972* (Allen Lane, The Penguin Press, 1988)

Garvin Tom, *Preventing the Future: Why was Ireland so poor for so long?* (Gill & Macmillan, 2004)

Grantham, Bill, 'Craic in a box: Commodifying and exporting the Irish pub', published in *Continuum: Journal of Media & Cultural Studies*, Vol. 23, 2009, Issue 2

Higgins, Michael D. *Renewing the Republic* (Liberties Press, 2011)

Hourigan, Niamh, *Rule-Breakers: Why 'Being There' Trumps 'Being Fair' in Ireland* (Gill Books, 2015)

Hourihane, Ann Marie, *She Moves Through the Boom* (Sitric Books, 2000)

Inglis, Tom [ed.], *Are the Irish Different?* (Manchester University Press, 2014)

Kiberd, Declan, *Inventing Ireland: The Literature of a Modern Nation* (Jonathan Cape, 1995)

Killeen, Richard, *Ireland: 1001 Things You Need to Know* (Atlantic Books, 2017)

Kostick, Conor, *Strongbow: The Norman Invasion of Ireland* (The O'Brien Press, 2013)

Laughlin, Jim, *Ireland: The Emigrant Nursery and the World Economy* (Cork University Press, 1994)

Lee, J.J., *Ireland 1912-1985: Politics and Society* (Cambridge University Press, 1989)

McGahern, John, *Memoir*, (Faber and Faber 2005)

McLysaght, Emer and Breen, Sarah, *Oh My God What a Complete Aisling The Novel* (Gill Books, 2017)

Maher, Eamon, O'Brien, Eugene, *Tracing the Cultural Legacy of Irish Catholicism: From Galway to Cloyne and Beyond* (Manchester University Press, 2017)

Moran, Albert and Keane, Michael, *Cultural Adaptation* (Routledge, 2013)

Okorie, Melatu Uche, *This Hostel Life* (Skein Press, 2018)

O'Hagan, John & O'Toole, Francis, *The Economy of Ireland, Policy-Making in a Global Context* (Palgrave 2017, 13th edition)

O'Toole, Fintan [ed.], Marshall, Catherine and Walshe, Eibhear [associate eds], *Modern Ireland in 100 Artworks* (Royal Irish Academy, 2016)

O'Toole, Fintan, *Ship of Fools: How Stupidity and Corruption Sank the Celtic Tiger* (Faber & Faber Ltd, 2009)

Roche, William K., O'Connell, Philip J. & Prothero, Andrea, *Austerity and recovery in Ireland: Europe's Poster Child and the Great Recession* (Oxford University Press, 2016)

Shannon, William V, *The American Irish: A Political and Social Portrait* (University of Massachusetts Press, 1989)

Thomson, David, *Woodbrook* (Vintage, 1994)

Wren, Maev-Ann, *Unhealthy State: Anatomy of a Sick Society* (New Island, 2003)

INDEX